A BIBLIOGRAPHY FOR *AFTER JEWS AND ARABS*

Before you start to read this book, take this moment to think about making a donation to punctum books, an independent non-profit press,

@ https://punctumbooks.com/support/

If you're reading the e-book, you can click on the image below to go directly to our donations site. Any amount, no matter the size, is appreciated and will help us to keep our ship of fools afloat. Contributions from dedicated readers will also help us to keep our commons open and to cultivate new work that can't find a welcoming port elsewhere. Our adventure is not possible without your support.

Vive la Open Access.

Fig. 1. Hieronymus Bosch, *Ship of Fools* (1490–1500)

A BIBLIOGRAPHY FOR *AFTER JEWS AND ARABS*. Copyright © 2021 by Ammiel Alcalay. This work carries a Creative Commons BY-NC-SA 4.0 International license, which means that you are free to copy and redistribute the material in any medium or format, and you may also remix, transform and build upon the material, as long as you clearly attribute the work to the authors (but not in a way that suggests the authors or punctum books endorses you and your work), you do not use this work for commercial gain in any form whatsoever, and that for any remixing and transformation, you distribute your rebuild under the same license. http://creativecommons.org/licenses/by-nc-sa/4.0/

First published in 2021 by dead letter office, BABEL Working Group, an imprint of punctum books, Earth, Milky Way.
https://punctumbooks.com

The BABEL Working Group is a collective and desiring-assemblage of scholar-gypsies with no leaders or followers, no top and no bottom, and only a middle. BABEL roams and stalks the ruins of the post-historical university as a multiplicity, a pack, looking for other roaming packs with which to cohabit and build temporary shelters for intellectual vagabonds. We also take in strays.

"Behind the Scenes: Before *After Jews and Arabs*" by Ammiel Alcalay, was first published (in a slightly different from) in *Memories of Our Future*, copyright © 1999 by Ammiel Alcalay. Reprinted with the permission of City Lights Books, www.citylights.com

ISBN-13: 978-1-953035-34-9 (print)
ISBN-13: 978-1-953035-35-6 (ePDF)

DOI: 10.21983/P3.0314.1.00

LCCN: 2021931014
Library of Congress Cataloging Data is available from the Library of Congress

Book design: Vincent W.J. van Gerven Oei
Cover image: Al-Mutanabbi Street, Baghdad. Photo by Sinan Antoon, used with permission.

spontaneous acts of scholarly combustion

HIC SVNT MONSTRA

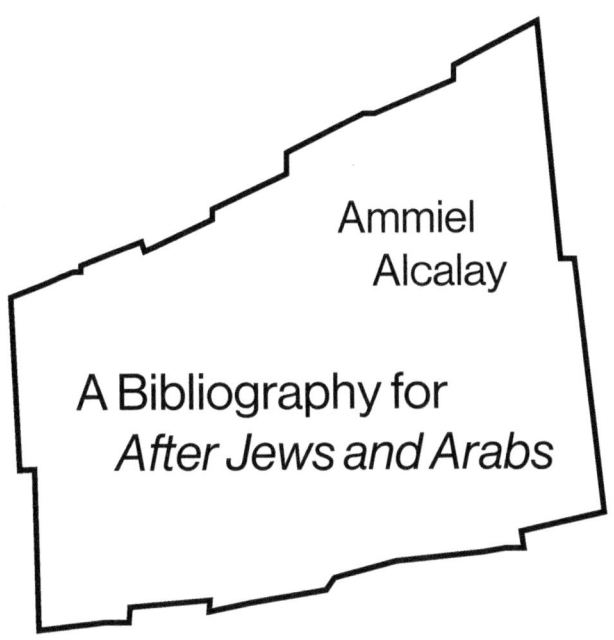

Ammiel Alcalay

A Bibliography for *After Jews and Arabs*

*To the booksellers of al-Mutanabbi Street in Baghdad
and to booksellers everywhere*

Contents

Acknowledgments	xiii
A Bibliography for *After Jews and Arabs*: A Brief Introduction	17
A Poetics of Bibliography	23
Behind the Scenes: Before *After Jews and Arabs*	39
Bibliography for Ammiel Alcalay, *After Jews & Arabs: Remaking Levantine Culture* (Minneapolis: University of Minnesota Press, 1993)	67

Acknowledgments

The seeds of this project began when I first met Eileen Joy in 2013 at a BABEL Working Group conference, "Critical/Liberal/ Arts," at The Graduate Center, CUNY, where I presented a talk actually called "From the Cairo Genizah to Diane di Prima's Garage." Little did I know just how clearly those lines would converge — as I write this, it has been only about three months since Diane's passing on October 25, 2020, and I find myself one of her literary executors.

Just a few months after the 2013 BABEL conference, I found myself recruiting Mary Catherine Kinniburgh, a potential new student in the PhD Program in English coming in, ostensibly, as a medievalist with experience in book history and map-making. By the time she finished her brilliant dissertation, mainly focusing on poets' libraries as unique repositories of knowledge, she had spent quite a bit of time in Diane's garage, cataloguing her unique occult library and, in many ways, inspiring me to think more deeply about what, exactly, I had on my hands in the bibliography enclosed in this book.

Back at the conference, when I first explained the circumstances of the bibliography's non-publication in my 1993 book *After Jews and Arabs: Remaking Levantine Culture* to Eileen, her immediate response was: "We'll publish it!" Buoyed by her initial enthusiasm, I set about putting it in order, before one thing after another kept intervening. Although years passed, finally, we've arrived! I want to express my sincere thanks to Eileen for her continued support and excitement about this project, as well as her clear and precise editing ideas throughout. I also want to thank Vincent W.J. van Gerven Oei of punctum books for his help in all phases of the project, particularly for its design and cover, itself a saga of sorts.

In all my work on 20th/21st-century archival materials related to *Lost & Found: The CUNY Poetics Document Initiative*, I have always kept in mind and emphasized in my teaching the precarious nature of archives and of various living repositories of cultural memory, with the very immediate examples of Iraq and Bosnia at hand, prefigured by the shadow Palestine casts over so much of my work. For some time, my intention had been to dedicate this project to the booksellers of al-Mutanabbi Street, the street of the booksellers in Baghdad. It is the former San Francisco bookseller Beau Beausoleil who began the traveling solidarity art project "al-Mutanabbi Street Starts Here," as a means of paying homage to those great purveyors of knowledge and art, following a car bomb attack in 2007 that wounded over one hundred and killed over thirty people on that venerable street.

But in setting out to find the right image for the cover of the book, circumstances further revealed the elusive nature of the cultural record. I had hoped for an older photo and got in touch with Andras Riedlmayer, the Bibliographer in Islamic Art and Architecture at Harvard's Fine Arts Library; Andras, in turn, contacted Jeff Spurr, formerly the Cataloger for Islamic Arts at the same library. Both Andras and Jeff had been deeply involved in international efforts to not only rebuild archives and libraries in both Bosnia and Iraq but, just as importantly, to document the destruction that had taken place. Through Andras I was led to Prof. Ian Johnson of Robert Gordon University in Scotland and, ultimately, to Ibrahim al-Rajab, Director of the long-standing al-Muthanna Library in Bagdad, but al-Rajab himself only had a few older photos of the shop and entreated Prof. Johnson to inform him should any other such images materialize. Jeff queried Dr. Saad Eskandar, former Director General of the Iraq National Library and Archive: again, we came up empty. We tried Matt Saba at MIT's Aga Khan Documentation Center but, because of the pandemic, the archive was closed. I thank all of them for their interest and their efforts.

I then turned to old and new friends at the Arab Image Foundation in Beirut, starting both in New York and Beirut. In New York, graduate student and novelist Brad Fox re-introduced me to Khaled Malas. By the time Khaled and I found each other, I was already in touch with Akram Zaatari, an old acquaintance—Akram did some searches for me and then suggested others to contact: I want to extend my heartfelt thanks to Khaled and Akram, both before and after the cataclysmic explosion of August 4, 2020, and also to Clémence Cottard Hachem and Yasmine Eid Sabbagh, for their courtesy and grace in responding to my queries. I asked others who sent me further: my thanks to Orit Bashkin, Khaled al-Hilly, and Parine Jaddo.

After all this, I realized I ought to ask an old friend, Sinan Antoon, who was from Baghdad. When I say "old friend," I don't think I exaggerate when I figure we must have met in the 9th or 10th century, either in Baghdad, working on a translation during the Abbasid period, or in al-Andalus, when the action moved west, perhaps poring over a newly circulating text or listening to a poet perform. And, indeed, after all the searches and queries, Sinan sent me a photo of al-Mutanabbi Street that he himself took, a photo that precisely captured the active spirit of the street I had hoped to portray, and this picture is now integrated into the cover of the book. Thank you Sinan!

While the bibliography has purposefully remained frozen in time and had not been updated since 1993, Eileen's eagle eye revealed various inconsistences, missing dates, lack of page numbers and various other bibliographical snafus. Faced with the task of chasing down references of titles I once held in hand, some of them forty years ago, I prepared myself for the worst. In doing so I asked Peter Cole, someone very familiar with this terrain, if he would be kind enough to track down some references once I narrowed them down. Incredibly, once I had gone through everything, I only had one question for Peter, the publication date of a collection of poems by David Onkineirah, a very obscure 16th-century poet who doesn't even show up on an internet search. Of course, Peter found the date I needed. I also want to thank Sami Shalom Chetrit, Chris Clarke, David Larsen, and Oyku Tekten for chasing down a detail here and there. Many thanks to Judah Rubin who carefully perused the project at various stages and found various missing data. And, lastly, my thanks to Miriam Nichols, for helping to remap my own geography and see older sites with new eyes.

Ammiel Alcalay
January 14, 2021

A Bibliography for *After Jews and Arabs*: A Brief Introduction

After Jews and Arabs: Remaking Levantine Culture was completed in 1989 and published in 1993 by the University of Minnesota Press after close to five years of contentious give and take with a number of other academic presses. The book was the first attempt in English, and possibly any other language, to fully recalibrate the relationship between Jews and Arabs within an "old world" geography centered on the Mediterranean, while taking into account a chronology that acknowledged and reached both backwards and forwards, from the pre-Islamic period to the present, a time when the question of Palestine largely came to define the relationship between Jews and Arabs. Embedded within a literary and cultural journey drawn from close to a dozen languages across this time and space, *After Jews and Arabs* also drew on a vast array of other sources: from architectural accounts of the creation of new cities like Fustat and Baghdad, to fragments of early medieval bills of lading and letters written by merchants drawn from the Cairo *genizah*; from covert Judeo-Spanish translations during the Inquisition, to accounts of the destruction of Palestinian villages in 1948; from contemporary acts of resistance to cultural assimilation by Jews writing in Arabic, to the revolutionary context of the first Palestinian *intifadah*.

The decision to write *After Jews and Arabs* came following several years of work, from the late 1970s to the mid-1980s, with the extraordinary polymath Eduard Roditi (1910–1992) who, unfortunately, died prior to the appearance of my book. Our aim in that project was to create a massive anthology by gathering writing by Jews from the pre-Islamic period to the then present, encompassing an enormous variety of materials, including literary, folkloric, scientific, exegetic, historical, and political works. When a major university press rejected our project on the grounds of not understanding the relationship between Arabic and Spanish aspects of Jewish culture, I realized that much work needed to be done. In some sense, *After Jews and Arabs* can be considered an elaborate introduction, along with a sampler of translated texts, for an anthology that never came to pass. And, in fact, still hasn't come to pass, at least not in the way we conceptualized it. The work closest in spirit, my own 1996 anthology *Keys to the Garden*,[1] presents only the briefest chronological span, from the 1960s to the 1980s, and only literary texts.

At this remove, the most innovative aspects of *After Jews and Arabs* — and those that elicited both the most resistance and the most excitement — have to do with three things. First, the willingness to isolate qualities that seemed to hold true across a drastically variable range of political, economic, and communal conditions within the framework of the geographic and chronological range I had outlined: qualities I defined as mobility, diversity, autonomy, and translatability. Next: the audacity to actually contextualize and test the legitimacy of these qualities through a vast bibliography, some areas of which I could not claim *absolute* expertise in. Finally, and this unquestionably is the aspect that elicited the deepest resistance to the book, the necessity of framing and exploring the past in the context of the

---

1 Ammiel Alcalay, *Keys to the Garden: New Israeli Writing* (San Francisco: City Lights Books, 1996).

present relationship of Jews and Arabs as made manifest by the issue of Palestine.

In the course of this work and its afterlife, in addition to making visible the culture it focused on, *After Jews and Arabs* certainly played a key role in helping to decenter the conventional western European canon and chronology. While shifting the medieval focus back to al-Andalus and, back of that, to the Abbasid Caliphate and earlier routes of knowledge transmission, the book also more squarely placed the contemporary period of Jewish history in the Middle East in the settings of colonization and decolonization, as opposed to the conventional nomenclature of the time, with all of its attendant ideological baggage, of "development" and "modernization." By now several generations of younger scholars have taken up discrete aspects of the larger tableau presented in *After Jews and Arabs* and the subject has actually become a legitimate field of knowledge in which certain prior and prevailing assumptions, often racist and exclusionary at core, no longer have footing, or at least no longer pass uncontested. At the same time, crucial and far-reaching projects involving the translation of Arabic literature, and some medieval Hebrew literature, have come to fruition. In general, both through scholarly texts and works aimed at a more general readership, the kind of apoplectic response elicited by the subject from supposedly well-informed academics and arbiters of permissible knowledge just thirty or thirty-five years ago seems, thankfully, to have become an embarrassment. Yet, at the same time, enormous gaps remain in both general knowledge and the more ready availability of key texts in translation.

While my own work has apparently gone in very different directions, at core the question of historical contextualization has remained central to whatever I'm engaged with. This, it seems to me, is a primary reason for wanting to go back and publish the original bibliography for *After Jews and Arabs*, left out of the 1992 book publication due to space issues. Publication of the bibliography for scholarly and other use, as important as that may be, is not the only reason to bring it out now, over twenty-five years after the fact. The bibliography itself is a pre-digital creation and, as such, has a lot to say methodologically and otherwise, particularly to younger scholars either born digital or still skirting the textual/digital divide, particularly as our ways of accessing information from the past continue to change.

Mine was a bibliography largely composed through card catalogues; open stacks; smaller, more manageable collections; and used or antiquarian bookshops, as well as through a large network of informants based in different languages, geographical sites, and particular human and political experience. Unquestionably, more than some of that residue remains in the very choice and organization of the items included. While providing a personal journey through some of these methodological issues, my prefatory essay "A Poetics of Bibliography" (see below) also points to the wider nets we, as scholars, need to throw out to our students and readers to provide guidance for how some of this older experience can be assessed and transmitted.

My decision to further contextualize the bibliography with the chapter after this one, "Behind the Scenes: Before *After Jews and Arabs*," an essay originally written in the late 1990s, and appearing in *Memories of Our Future*,[2] a book of selected essays that came out in 1999, has to do with a certain discursive impasse we have come to in public expression, particularly in an academic context. As the initiatory rites of academic certification have become more technical, technocratic, and professionalized, issues of authority and judgment have become almost completely occluded. On the one hand, authority and judgment have been relegated to the realm of the "authoritarian" and the "judgmental" but, importantly, without ever exposing and laying bare the still very existent mechanisms under which authority and judgment take place. The general refusal to engage in true differences of position outside a highly circumscribed spectrum and, rarely, if ever, engage in actual debate while continually preaching to the choir, has caused irreparable harm to our

---

[2] Ammiel Alcalay, *Memories of Our Future: Selected Essays, 1982–1999* (San Francisco: City Lights Books, 1999).

intellectual and human capacities, pulling the reins back just as we get ready to take off.

The genesis of "Behind the Scenes: Before *After Jews and Arabs*" was an attempt to engage detractors of the book in an open debate, in order to try and advance the state of knowledge and scholarship and bring the issues out into the open. After many proposals to magazines, journals, and other venues, no one was willing to even consider hosting a forum in which the kinds of positions staked out in the anonymous reader reports and my response to them could be signed, owned, and openly discussed as genuinely contentious issues with larger structural and political implications both in and out of academia. My decision to, as it were, "go public" without permission and publish the anonymous reader reports, was a move, needless to say, not without certain risk. While it has been hard to calculate the actual fallout, I have never published another book with a university press, even though I am constantly called on as a reader (who, I might add, always waives "anonymity"), or as a writer of blurbs. At the same time, I think my exposure of the process remains a very useful example of how to stake out and hold a position, how to actually make a scholarly argument based on the refutation of misrepresentation, an exercise too rarely available in our highly encoded and separated camps, each with its own assumptions, rhetoric, jargon, and modes of membership.

While "A Poetics of Bibliography" is both speculative and personal, drawing on and marking my own historical experience, "Behind the Scenes: Before *After Jews and Arabs*," is forensic and analytical, exposing all the contradictions of my detractors in light of the proofs I bring to bear on the argument. As to the bibliography itself, my hope is that some of the residue I mention previously, of the actual individual and collective work involved in everything compiled there, might emerge as a form of world-making, an offering that provides an example of how materials from the past can be arranged to perforate the caul too often obscuring our vision, preventing us from seeing a ground we can actually stand on. My hope also is that the materials gathered in this volume can work as a kind of methodological tool kit, allowing readers with differing levels of familiarity to find ways to engage with each section for different purposes and towards different ends and thus carry this long dormant burden and lode further afield.

1

A Poetics of Bibliography

1. The Long Haul, or "a saturation job"

I began compiling this bibliography in the late 1970s, as my interest was drawn, for a variety of reasons, to those parts of the world it encompasses. The process of thought, fieldwork, research, and writing that brought the bibliography to completion, and the writing that emerged from it (in the form of my book *After Jews and Arabs: Remaking Levantine Culture*,[1] as well as various other books, projects, and activities), lasted somewhere between twelve and eighteen years, certainly enough to qualify for what poet Charles Olson called "a saturation job." As he put it in what was later published as *A Bibliography on America for Ed Dorn,* a document Olson originally prepared in the mid-1950s for his student, Edward Dorn, as a course of study for him at and *after* his studies at Black Mountain College:

> Best thing to do is to dig one thing or place or man until you yourself know more abt that than is possible to any other man. It doesn't matter whether it's Barbed Wire or Pemmican or Paterson or Iowa. But exhaust it. Saturate it. Beat it.

---

1 Ammiel Alcalay, *After Jews and Arabs: Remaking Levantine Culture* (Minneapolis: University of Minnesota Press, 1993).

> And then u know everything else very fast: one
> saturation job (it might take 14 years). And you're in, forever.[2]

Olson's text first appeared as a pamphlet published by Donald M. Allen, editor of the ground-breaking and influential 1960 *New American Poetry,* an anthology that brought poets who knew of each other through letter writing but had only appeared in very small, often self-published magazines, to a much wider audience. Many poets and writers coming of age in the early 1960s discovered these poets through that anthology and themselves went on to become participants in the counterculture of the mid- to late 1960s. The 1964 *Bibliography* pamphlet inaugurated Allen's Four Seasons Foundation and its Writing series, an important publication that would continue for decades and later grow into several other small press ventures under Allen's editorship. All of this was part of a burgeoning revolt against the Cold War culture of containment and its particular manifestation in the academic administration of knowledge that was largely in service of state power and imperialist policies.

Right at the beginning of his bibliography, Olson wrote:

> Assumptions: (1) that *politics & economics* (that
> is, agriculture, fisheries, capital and
> labor) are like love (can only be
> individual experience) and therefore,
> as they have been presented (again,
> like love) are not much use, that is
> any of the study of the books about
>
> (2) that *sociology,* without exception, is
> a lot of shit — produced by people
> who are the most dead of all, history
> as politics or economics each being at

---

[2] Charles Olson, *A Bibliography on America for Ed Dorn* (San Francisco: Four Seasons Foundation, 1964), 13.

least events and laws, not this dreadfull
beast, some average and statistic[3]

Encountering this as a teenager in the late 1960s, I can't say I'm sure I fully understood it but I somehow still knew what it meant. Unquestionably, though, if I thought of a "bibliography," I thought of this very idiosyncratic document. And it was clearly a creative act, not simply a dutiful compilation. The question of "sociology" so boldly stated, was only fully clarified years later when I encountered the following astounding statistic in Christopher Simpson's essential but almost unknown 1994 masterpiece, *The Science of Coercion: Communication Research and Psychological Warfare 1945–1960,* stating that a 1952 National Science Foundation "report shows that 96 percent of all reported federal funding for social science at that time was drawn from the U.S. military."[4]

II. Identity, Kinship, Propaganda

What, one might well and justifiably ask, does any of this have to do with the first publication of an extensive bibliography that should have been part of a book published over twenty-five years ago, a book that, as I then wrote in the introduction, explores: "the relationships between Jews and Arabs on the literary, cultural, social, and political planes [...] and the relationship of the Jew to the Arab within him or herself"?[5] Coming of age in the late 1960s I was acutely aware, of course, that peoples and histories had been suppressed, that sources were ignored, that propaganda was meant to force people into acting against their own best interests in the most destructive ways imaginable.

As I participated in public life quite vocally, also imbibing all the sources of the times — from music and underground papers

3   Ibid., 3.
4   Christopher Simpson, *The Science of Coercion: Communication Research and Psychological Warfare, 1945–1960* (New York: Oxford University Press, 1994), 52.
5   Alcalay, *After Jews and Arabs,* 27.

to pirated editions and small press publications—the cultural heroes I held close to heart came from another era but formed the basis of the one I was witness to and participant in: poets like Charles Olson and Vincent Ferrini, Diane di Prima and LeRoi Jones/Amiri Baraka, musicians like Sun Ra, Albert Ayler, Ornette Coleman, and Cecil Taylor. Texts such as Olson's *Call Me Ishmael* and Jones/Baraka's *Blues People* showed me that history could not only be written differently but that, as Olson put it, knowledge could be "made active." These texts themselves harkened back to the more idiosyncratic scholarship of W.E.B. DuBois's *The Souls of Black Folk,* D.H. Lawrence's *Studies in Classic American Literature,* William Carlos Williams's *In the American Grain,* Edward Dahlberg's *Can These Bones Live,* and Muriel Rukeyser's *Willard Gibbs.* Musicians like Ayler, Coleman, and Taylor enacted the upper limits of form, *and* recall—demonstrating that there *were* ways back to forgotten melodies one never knew. Later, I would be led to musicologist Victor Zuckerkandl through poet Nathaniel Mackey, and Mackey's profound formulation: "Music is wounded kinship's last resort,"[6] a major theme of *After Jews and Arabs,* and all its related projects.

As the possibilities opened up by the mass movements of the 1960s were suppressed and assassinations piled up, full-scale structural readjustment brought deindustrialization, mass incarceration, and much deeper social atomization. With all the potential freedom built on the ground of those movements, to impose control, state resources and propaganda mechanisms steered the necessary undertaking of identity formation directed at the reinstatement of a more just historical equilibrium toward the very divisive free-for-all that identity politics now seems to have become. This was, by no means, a simple or straightforward process: it went hand in hand with counterintelligence operations (in the form of COINTELPRO, the counter intelligence

---

6 Nathaniel Mackey, "Sound and Sentiment, Sound and Symbol," quoted in Charles Bernstein, ed., *The Politics of Poetic Form: Poetry and Public Policy* (New York: Roof Books, 1990), 88. Also see Andrew R. Mossin, "The Song Sung in a Strange Land: An Interview with Nathaniel Mackey," *The Iowa Review* 44, no. 3 (Winter 2014/15): 172–92, particularly 174–75..

program initiated by the FBI in the mid-1950s, a series of covert and illegal projects meant to disrupt, subvert, and destroy certain US political organizations), and various other forms of coercion forcing people to divide along various lines of identity through disinformation campaigns and institutionalized forms of treatment according to category of person. But it was also self-imposed, even championed, by those very people justifiably seeking more representation. As the late Egyptian thinker and economist Samir Amin so cogently and repeatedly illustrated, the acceptance of "difference" in place of equality under the law and liberation is, ultimately, an anti-democratic subterfuge that perpetuates structures of subjugation.

From 1972 to 1980, as Melani McCallister brilliantly depicts in her 2005 book *Epic Encounters: Culture, Media, and U.S. Interests in the Middle East since 1945,* the US media obliterated the Vietnam Veteran-led anti-war movement, turning the soldiers who had heroically resisted their roles into cowardly and disposable dependents while promoting the heroism of Israeli soldiers and forging new archetypes of hero and terrorist that would both create and inhabit the popular imagination before and after 9/11. As the rust set in and the industrial base of the country collapsed, people were taught to take pride in their ethnic heritage, and the example of Israel openly led the way, through the evangelical movement and various other means, in definitively shaping the parameters of US foreign *and* domestic policy, deeply internalizing and solidifying policies that had still been in contention since at least the beginning of the 20th century.

This was the context of the late 1970s in which I set out to investigate "my own" ancestral places and sources, since I was that very particular thing: first generation "American," barely born in the country but embracing it like the home it certainly was, despite, despite everything. Part of the pull back to the Old World had to do with unrepresented histories, familial mythology, and those unique forms of propaganda that only families seem to generate: knowing that there was something back then and there in al-Andalus, but not seeing it represented anywhere. The circle of that sense and sentiment was squared upon meeting Moroccan and Iraqi-born Jewish Black Panthers in Jerusalem. Over time, these early forays led to the "saturation job" resulting in *After Jews & Arabs,* and the worlds its formerly unpublished bibliography contains.

III. Worldmaking

The world I set out to investigate had no label, no category connecting to the present or tying various pasts together. European Zionist norms dictated and subsumed any other possibilities: Arab Jews were considered a folkloric category at best, a social problem at worst. Communities that had once co-existed in an autonomous space, who spoke the same language, were now simply assumed to be eternal enemies, whether they were called Iraqi, Palestinian, Syrian, Lebanese, Moroccan, Algerian, Libyan, Tunisian, Egyptian, or Yemeni. The bitter irony of one of the region's unsung optimists, Eliyahu Eliachar, came out clearly in the titles of two of his books: *Existing with Jews* and *Living with Palestinians.* Having undergone a multi-year effort with polymath poet, biographer, and translator Edouard Roditi to create a massive anthology of writings by Jews from pre-Islamic times in Southern Arabia to the 20th century, only to have it rejected out of hand by a major university press because they didn't see any correlation between its Arabic and Spanish-Andalusian aspects, I saw that if there were a stage to be set, I would have to set it. Much work needed to be done to even create the framework in which such obscured correlations could become more visible.

Since there was no extant discipline through which a project like that anthology or *After Jews and Arabs* could be undertaken, I set about familiarizing myself with a vast range of materials drawn from various subjects, including history and historiography; anthropology, ethnography, and ethnomusicology; political economy and geography; linguistics; philosophy; and the history of science and technology. In effect, I needed to seek both the training *and* a basic bibliographic outline to create scholarship for which there was, as yet, no clearly defined field.

At the same time, an endeavor of this kind inevitably bumped head on into the question of information overload.

One of the earliest articulations of this sense of overload comes in the 1903 introduction to *The New Empire* by Brooks Adams, a key source for Charles Olson, when Adams remarks upon the plethora of information that a researcher or thinker aiming to synthesize materials into general laws or concepts is confronted with: "the mass of material is accumulating rapidly. Libraries are no longer able to buy and catalogue the volumes which appear, and he who would read intelligently must first learn to eliminate."[7] After resigning from the Office of War Information in 1944, in correspondence with anthropologist and co-worker Ruth Benedict, and later poet Robert Creeley, Olson formed his unique concept of the "postmodern," based very much on Adams's concern with information overload and the need, as Adams put it, to move from particularities to generalities: "A fact in itself has no significance; neither have a thousand facts. What gives facts their value is their relation to each other; for when enough have been collected to suggest a sequence of cause and effect, a generalization can be made."[8] In a 1946 letter to Benedict, Olson writes: "It is my feeling that the record of fact is become of first importance for us lost in a sea of question [...]. In New History, the act of the observer, if his personality is of count, is before, in the collection of the material. This is where we will cut the knot. I think if you burn the facts long and hard enough in yourself as crucible, you'll come to the few facts that matter, and then fact can be fable again."[9] Olson's sense of "fable" here goes directly to its root: to speak, say, narrate, create a narrative.

In this sense, the bibliography published here for the first time, and excluded in 1992 from *After Jews and Arabs* for space reasons, is an essential part of the narrative, not simply a refer-

---

7   Brooks Adams, *The New Empire* (New York; The MacMillan Company, 1903), xviii.
8   Ibid.
9   Ammiel Alcalay, *a little history* (Los Angeles and New York: re: public / UpSet Press, 2012), 68–69.

ence tool, but a constituent element, a creative act penetrating the fog to make available the ground upon which other realities can be imagined and enacted. In a lecture on Olson's bibliography and its meaning for him, Ed Dorn comments that,

> the value for a student in a well-conceived bibliography is not in the bibliography's comprehension, or completeness, if such a completion were possible, but in the engagement of certain of its — I don't want to say "genes." But in the engagement of certain of its — I'd like to say here that the lighthearted depreciation of some of Olson's sources on the basis that some of them are dated — for instance, I've heard this charged against the Pleistocene work — or not up to date, leave me cold, and unimpressed. The value of a working instructional bibliography lies in its net of connections. It isn't concerned with the latest so- called "corrections" and insights of the latest worker, or the latest hot number. The value for a student in a well-conceived bibliography is not in the bibliography's comprehension, but in the engagement of certain of its genes....[10]

This passage describes perfectly why I've felt that pursuing publication of this "old" bibliography, purposely *not* updated but frozen in the time of its use, made sense to me and has further implications, given that it illustrates "the collection of the materials" and embodies the "net of connections."

And that leads into further methodological issues: in a different context altogether, I recently wrote that the wars in the former Yugoslavia seem to me to be the last prominent wars to have taken place in print, and the coincidence between the completion of my bibliography and the date of those wars, 1992 to 1995, is not happenstance, given that I was working in both realms simultaneously. While this is not the place for an extended investigation of the implications of this assertion, suffice

---

10 Edward Dorn, *Charles Olson Memorial Lectures,* ed. Lindsey M. Freer, Lost & Found: The CUNY Poetics Document Initiative, Series 3, No. 5 (New York: Center for the Humanities, 2012), 12.

it to say that what characterized my work in both areas has been the relationship between experience and accumulated as well as emerging print knowledge, with the assumption of a relatively stable material archive. The relative nature of stability may be more obvious in one case, given the condition of war in the former Yugoslavia, but the same tension between what is lived and what becomes known through documentary sources is evident throughout *After Jews and Arabs* and its attendant offshoots, in which daily political events and relationships between actual "Jews" and actual "Arabs," and my own experience in and of them, became the filter though which the historical knowledge I explored was sifted. Waiting in line at a tiny kiosk for music cassettes from Iraq and Algeria brought back from Paris; seeing a once great musician in tatters begging in the marketplace; watching smoke rise from burning tire barricades near Jerusalem's grim housing projects; taking testimony from imprisoned Palestinian children, seeing people dragged in shackles from the torture chamber just a hundred yards from the Central Post Office; standing in vigil with friends whose relatives were starving in the Lebanese camps war because of an Israeli Navy blockade; seeing the collective courage of a truly popular uprising during the first Intifada: all had to be weighed in the balance — like the feather of justice — with every book or document I encountered.

IV. "the dance of freedom"

My sense, in every way, is that we now face acute challenges in the attempt to reinstate what Siraj Ahmed in his brilliant *Archaeology of Babel: The Colonial Foundations of the Humanities,* calls suppressed "discursive practices" that have been effaced and displaced by both centralized textual and state power. My own struggle to weigh textual and archival materials against the unfolding present I was experiencing is very much a part of these "discursive practices." In moving across the textual/digital divide I think we also have to consider some of our own very basic discursive practices, as researchers, scholars, writers, and artists. One of the primary methodological or procedural issues I now see among generations born digital is that, while it is much easier to find something already identified in particular, it has become that much harder to find something one *isn't* looking for. Chance encounters leading down unknown paths have become exceedingly hard to experience. Without rarifying the pre-digital age, this process hearkens back to all kinds of different material situations: open stack libraries, antiquarian bookshops, personal collections, all of which must be physically looked at in markedly different circumstances rather than in solitary reception through a screen. In other words, in such a search for something one is looking for, one encounters many more things one *wasn't* looking for but which may be of enormous use and value. Even the compilation of a bibliography such as mine would be that much harder now. Just perusing it in the present already marks it an artifact of an earlier era, curious, possibly useful, but very difficult to fully decode.

Initial reactions to suppress publication of *After Jews and Arabs* were fiercely ideological and explicitly racist. I wonder, at this remove, whether a book like mine would presently even reach the point of contention depicted in the next text in this volume, "Behind the Scenes: Before *After Jews & Arabs*," despite this contention taking place behind the closed doors of anonymous reader reports. This is not to imply that I don't believe such attempts at suppression no longer take place but I think the scene has shifted considerably, to the point where accommodation to certain more sanctioned forms of critique have not only become permissible but desired, as a means of managing difference through containment and limitation. In other words, self-censorship, compliance and, ultimately, the naturalization of generic codes, boundaries and limitations, have all helped obviate some of the kinds of ideological conflicts depicted in such raw manner in "Behind the Scenes."

I know that, in my case, I haven't published with a university press since, partly from choice but surely also because I had been thought of as a loose cannon, someone who might do something as rash as try to goad my censors into an open debate by publishing their anonymous reports. The absence of such debate, not only in my particular case but in so many others, has truly been a loss for public discourse and the advancement or refinement of thought, and it allows the next best thing — the follower, the imitator whose door was opened by the innovator — to take precedence. All of this upholds the most superficial individuality by reproducing a kind of celebrity while militating against solidarity and the idea that such work is, of necessity, collaborative: such collaboration, of course, doesn't just take place among the living.

And one can multiply instances of such processes in so many different contexts, forcing culture and thought to either conform, or turn in on itself. And this goes across every field of knowledge, perhaps most alarmingly, in the sciences. How much hasn't been articulated or discovered because of these control structures? How many truly ambitious ideas have gone untried because of the internalization of so many codes of behavior? How many deeper and significant shifts have been thwarted? Clearly, the scope of *After Jews and Arabs* was not something one person could or should realistically have undertaken — and yet, I went ahead with it.

The stakes seem to me considerably higher than one instance, and my own efforts matter not just because they were mine, but because they were efforts. In one of my true and tried "textbooks," *Investigative Poetry,* poet, journalist, and musician Ed Sanders writes about "Investigative Eleutherarchs":

> Lawyers have a term: "to make law." You "make law" when you're involved in a case or an appeal which, as in Supreme Court decisions which have expanded the scope of personal freedom, opens up new human avenues.
>
> You make law.

Bards, in a similar way, "make reality," or, really, they make "freedom" or they create new modes of what we might term Eleutherarchy, or the dance of freedom.[11]

My intention in writing *After Jews and Arabs* was also to make a poet's book. But here, again, we have been subsumed, subjugated, and, finally, diminished by categories that do not serve our interests, our truly common sense. Poets have largely been made to think they no longer have the right to pursue anything bigger than themselves or can only lay the most partial claim to anything of the past, given the thorough indoctrination of "presentist" superiority. This kind of "progressive" ideology not only colonizes the past but severely limits what we allow our imaginations to activate and also curtails the unscripted alliances we might make with both the living and the dead.

While some version of the "commons" appears and reappears as an idealized and longed for site, it is too often simply a rhetorical gesture rather than a sustained intellectual or political practice. As poetry and poetics have become more and more institutionalized, and that institutionalization has become internalized, we have all but lost sight of the kind of disruption referred to by poet Robert Duncan when he wrote: "I have to break up orders, to loosen the bindings of my own conversions, for my art too constantly rationalizes itself, seeking to perpetuate itself as a conventional society. I am trying to keep alive our awareness of the dangers of my own convictions."[12]

In some sense, by revisiting this bibliography now, situating its value in method rather than content while contextualizing it as having come from a previous technological age, I am also unsettling its prior specific use and trying to understand what I might have learned from it. Going back to Olson, specifically his class notes for a course at Black Mountain College in 1956,

---

11 Ed Sanders, *Investigative Poetry* (New York: Spuyten Duyvil, 2018), 14.
12 Robert Duncan, "Man's Fulfillment in Order and Strife," in *Collected Essays and Other Prose*, ed. James A. Maynard (Berkeley and Los Angeles: University of California Press, 2014), 215.

the year I was born, and edited by Ann Charters as *The Special View of History,* we can see a definition of history embodying a kind of knowledge that almost seems diametrically opposed to the "saturation job." As Olson noted:

> There is no limit to what you can know. Or there is only in the sense that you don't find out or you don't seek to know. There is no truth at all, of course, in the modern velleity (the lowest degree of desire) that you can't know everything. It is literally true that you *have* to know everything. And for the simplest reason; that you do, by being alive.[13]

This refreshingly empowering concept seems a far cry from the diminished capacities we have been subjugated into by such theoretical abstractions as "power" or "bio-politics," and much closer to a concept articulated in an interview with composer and musician Cecil Taylor:

> If you have the opportunity to play for people all in different countries, one of the things you begin to discover is that people are — you can find oppressed people all over the world, therefore somewhere along the road you get the idea that it is certainly not about yourself. Any gift that you have is not about that at all. It's about a force that is about the ungiven, the uncreative. It is about the amorphous, and you are at best merely a vessel. And once you begin to understand that [...]. So in our small way what we attempt to do is to look and see and receive and become a sponge and attempt to make anything that exists as part of the palette to describe whatever it is we think we want to do. And what you want to do is to be as beautiful and as loving and as all-consuming as possible, so that the statement has many, many different implications

---

[13] Charles Olson, *The Special View of History,* ed. Ann Charters (Berkeley: Oyez, 1970), 29.

and it has many different levels. The only way to do that, it seems to me, is to research.¹⁴

V. Old Scholarship and its Future

As present conditions spectacularly move us into a future that jettisons more and more of the past, the activation of old scholarship remains a huge issue in the continuing transmission of knowledge and the sustainability of human relations outside models of consumption. Like the untapped energies of magnetic fields envisioned and made active by Nikola Tesla, the progenitor of electricity as we know it, our archives, libraries, personal collections, and memories contain vast resources that generally remain hidden, off-site, hard to access, intimidating. In the spirit of accessibility, the publication of this bibliography is an example and a record: an example of the kind of gathering that can create a new field of force, and the record of a struggle that, at least for the time being, ended in defeat but, nevertheless, may have much to demonstrate. The struggle depicts a historical juncture in which the political agency of a group of people particularly identified by their geographical and chronological commonality, embroiled in an untenable set of political constraints, made valiant attempts to mobilize themselves on the basis of the memory of that history. This is, of course, not an uncommon phenomenon but one that, in fact, is ever present across many historical junctures and moments, from uprisings and movements to revolutions and even counter-revolutions.

In *Charles Olson: The Last Lectures,* a group of faithful students took notes since Olson did not want to be recorded, and one of the key concepts he returned to again and again is what he called "the new illiteracy." At one point he says:

> In our post-pre-literate period you must get close to illiterate
> to be a human being

---

14   Chris Funkhauser, "Being Matter Ignited: An Interview with Cecil Taylor," *Hambone* 12 (1995): 19.

Maybe his wish *not* to be recorded was also a means of forcing his students to face this very condition. One of the last notes transcribed reads as follows:

> If you condition yrself to approach the mythology / poetry in words
> & letters
> & alphabets
> & the materials
>   on which they are inscribed
>   like you would a tree
>   or a rock
>   or a god
> *then* you will have directed yrself toward the future.[15]

How, exactly, are we to interpret this oddly prescient approach? As I have learned from my son's work in theoretical physics, cosmology, and natural philosophy, the cosmos is a place of infinite potential: it is only the imposed scarcity of planet earth under relatively more recent human reign that has made us think otherwise.[16] But as this reign becomes ever more rapacious, cataclysm seems inevitable. As the excesses of a technological civilization geared only towards pure extraction hurtle us toward mass die-offs, perhaps indigenous peoples and those who have remained closer to the earth will salvage something out of the rubble. We can get some sense of this, in a completely different context, from the great geographer Carl Sauer's "The End of the Ice Age and its Witnesses," a text that was very important for Olson and his embrace of Sauer's insistence that, to locate

---

15 John Cech, Oliver Ford, and Peter Rittner, eds., *Charles Olson in Connecticut: Last Lectures* (Iowa City: The Windhover Press, University of Iowa, 1974), 26. The lectures themselves were delivered in October and November of 1969, just months before Olson's death in January 1970.
16 Aram Alcalay, *Gravitation: A New Theoretical Paradigm* (New Hampshire: Gg Press, 2021).

any particular event, we must attempt, as faithfully as we can, to consider "the earth in all the time of human existence."[17]

Surely these bibliographies and archives and even the memories of them will fade like lost items from Babylonian libraries, the incinerated remains of repositories in contemporary Baghdad and Sarajevo, or from civilizations we don't even know existed. While it remains crucial to study the history of things as they become institutionalized — through the habits of language, the political economy of social structures, and so on — we need to remember that it is people who make things, including machines, and people who also make choices, or at least have the potential to make them. My own experience has shown me that even academic scholarship — no matter the apparent level of detachment — is, in almost all cases, highly personal. My case is no different, even though I came to the conclusion — in a wedding of rational thought and emotional clarity — that my geographical ambitions were misplaced, that I had, actually, been "at home" all along. While this has been a startling realization and somewhat difficult to handle on a personal level, the journey remains instructive and it is that which I hope this mixture of old scholarship (in the form of the bibliography), exposé (in the form of the trials and tribulations of the politics of publishing in the next chapter), and current thought (through this introduction), can offer. In that vein, this project seems very much like an offering to some as yet undefined entity that may simply be a feeling or a premonition based on what I have experienced and come to know, and it is in that spirit that I hope it will be taken further.

---

17 Carl O. Sauer, "Foreword to Historical Geography," *Annals of the Association of American Geographers* 31, no. 1 (March 1941): 24.

2

Behind the Scenes: Before *After Jews and Arabs*

The movement toward studies that went into what eventually became *After Jews and Arabs: Remaking Levantine Culture,* published in 1993, began — faintly — in the late 1970s, and picked up speed and intensity in the mid-1980s. One form of the manuscript was finished, as my doctoral dissertation, in 1988. The circumstances of that writing, I would like to think, were somewhat different than much of the academic writing I generally encounter, either as a reader or within formal academic contexts. In retrospect, I find that *After Jews and Arabs* is a book that has seriously been read by a lot of poets and used as the tool I had meant it to become, because it has a poetic and musical structure. Its most sensitive and intelligent assessment (written by Peter Lamborn Wilson) was, in fact, published in *Sulfur,* the journal edited by the poet and translator Clayton Eshleman, arguably the most important American literary editor of the past thirty-odd years. While my textual models included works like *Call Me Ishmael* by Charles Olson, *Can These Bones Live* by Edward Dahlberg, *The Shape of Time* by George Kubler, *The Souls of Black Folk* by W.E.B. Du Bois, *Blues People* by Amiri Baraka, *Genoa* by Paul Metcalf, and *My Emily Dickinson* by Susan Howe, there was a deeper echo that had to do with the modes in which "traditions" and "innovations" can be juxtaposed to stand out in relief. It was a musician, the guitar player Marc Ribot, who queried me about this and understood that I had in mind the kind of formal issues brought up by composers like Albert Ayler or Cecil Taylor. Such issues would include, for example, reference to a known refrain or blues phrase in a radically open improvisational composition.

At any rate, I was a writer (shades of the elated, belated, and painful declaration by William Carlos Williams, "I am a poet! I / am. I am. I am a poet, I reaffirmed, ashamed").[1] That is, the quality and design of the writing were as important to me as what it was I was trying to say. I was lucky enough to have the support and wisdom of teachers who were also writers and translators of the first order, particularly Allen Mandelbaum (most well known for his translations of Dante, Ovid, and Homer, but also a poet whose linguistic and cultural sensibility is unique on the American scene), Frederick Goldin (a powerful interpreter of the medieval Troubadours and Minnesangers), and Burton Pike (recognized, most recently, for his pioneering work on and translation of Robert Musil). During this period, I had spent close to seven years in Jerusalem where, ironically, I had forgotten just how narrowly circumscribed American cultural space was regarding any kind of alternative views on the intellectual, social, and political history of the Middle East in general and the relationship of Jews, Arabs, Palestinians, and Israelis in particular. This is where even starker shades of another declaration cast their distinct outline, in the form of Mahmoud Darwish's unequivocal lines: "Put it on record. / I am an Arab."[2] Framed within my own personal context, such a declaration might have seemed far-fetched, but within the collective endeavor I had undertaken — that is, an examination of, as I wrote in the preface to *After Jews and Arabs,* "the relationships between Jews and

---

1 William Carlos Williams, *Pictures from Breughel and Other Poems* (New York: New Directions, 1962), 120.
2 Mahmoud Darwish, *The Music of Human Flesh,* trans. Denys Johnson-Davies (London and Washington: Heinemann and Three Continents, 1980), 10.

Arabs on the literary, cultural, social, and political planes...and the relationship of the Jew to the Arab within him or herself,"[3] it came as a threat. In short, my manuscript began to circulate in an environment that was not only indisposed toward it formally but actually downright hostile toward it on ideological grounds.

Needless to say, attempts to get the manuscript published were met with enormous resistance. These attempts lasted close to five years before the book was finally accepted by the University of Minnesota Press. While this proved to be a very frustrating experience, I took umbrage in the fact that the vehement, vicious, and intellectually dishonest nature of the reactions to my work meant that it really was threatening and could actually effect change once it began to circulate. The bottom line boiled down to a very simple equation of power and authority: if my premises, assumptions, and conclusions gained in popularity, many of these people would simply no longer hold any legitimate authority in what they were teaching or writing without taking cognizance of my work or attempting to engage in a dialogue or a debate over it. If anything, it is this cowardly behavior that has most frustrated me. I feel that the field in which I am engaged — however one defines it, whether as Cultural, Middle Eastern, or Jewish Studies — has been very much impoverished by the absence of an open debate on *After Jews and Arabs*. I have tried, in a variety of ways, to ferret these anonymous critics out of their ivory bunkers and by-lines, but to no avail. After the Oslo Accords, an enormous victory for mainstream Zionism and a politically disastrous decision for the Palestinians, a new approach was taken. I was suddenly being asked to participate. It was quite comical to begin getting invitations for speaking engagements or article submissions from people who, only the week before, wouldn't have dreamed of asking me to do anything. I am not sure whether what follows (extracts from two of the original anonymous reader's reports, and my rebuttal to the second, more substantial report) will finally bring out the critics

3   Ammiel Alcalay, *After Jews and Arabs: Remaking Levantine Culture* (Minneapolis: University of Minnesota Press, 1993), 27.

to engage openly with my work but at least, in Mahmoud Darwish's words, it will be there for "the record." Without further ado, here is the first extract:

> This book does not represent new research but a very personal view of the situation of what the author calls "Mediterranean and Arab Jews." It is a rather strange combination of history, literary analysis and quotes from a variety of literature worked into a pastiche containing the author's own dislike of Israel, Zionism and Ashkenazic Jews. There is, therefore, no group of "specialists in the author's field" who could welcome its publication.
>
> There is a great deal of culling of quotations, but I would not call it scholarship. It is a highly romanticized work of the "picture of a vanished world" genre. The author does not mention by name the most important work on the major part of his many subjects, *The Jews of Islam* by Bernard Lewis. Since I didn't receive a copy of his notes, I don't know whether he quoted from it. Much of what Lewis, the outstanding scholar in the field, writes contradicts flatly statements by Alcalay about the socioeconomic status of the Jewish communities of which he writes.
>
> If one is interested in the personal views of the writer — I don't know who he is but I assume that he may be of Iraqi Jewish origin — it is a valid perspective on a little known subject. Not an important work in my view.
>
> The style is florid and at times unintelligible. The spelling is horrendous in places: the author hasn't learned the basic "i before e" rule, etc. The "organization" is such that I found it difficult to follow some of the author's arguments. What gives it some power, however, is the strong emotional component. The author feels the subject strongly.
>
> I cannot see this fitting into the publishing agenda of the Press. It is not a scholarly work nor is it a more personal work by a noted figure that would make it interesting to a broad public. It will be of interest primarily to people who want further ammunition to use against Israel although the author

sees his message as a broader critique of what modernity has done to the Middle East in general.

While I will let much of this go unremarked, I find the racist assumptions here to be most telling: that is, there seems to be some correlation in this reader's mind between his or her assumption that I am of Iraqi origin (which I am not, unless of course one goes back to the tenth century, in which case I might be, and which would only further prove many of the points I was trying to make in the book), and the "strong emotional component." I bring this up because it comes up, again and again. This first report, because of its brevity, must have relied on its author's reputation and authority in the field since there doesn't appear to be any need to even attempt proving its suppositions or claims. The writer of the next report, however, decided that my work posed such a threat that it needed to be misrepresented, in detail:

> The main goal of the ms. is to provide a new view of the historical relationship between Jews and Arabs on the literary, cultural, historical, social and political planes; to shed light on "the relationship of the Jew to the Arab within himself or herself"; to examine the relationship of the Near Eastern or Oriental Jew "to a native space, namely, the Levant." Although a great melange of evidence is marshalled for support, much of it is highly selective, some of it quite tendentious, and often it is grossly misinterpreted. (See my attached report).
>
> Although polemical works are always stimulating, I do not think this is a significant contribution to the field. The author tries to disarm potential criticism by claiming to be an amateur. But that does not relieve him from responsibility for knowing what has been done in the field. He certainly has read a great deal, but he has also missed a great deal. Many of the false or exaggerated claims would not have been made if he had gone further. (See my attached report).
>
> The dense style and the bombast preclude any general readership. Although this may appeal to some comparative literature people who have no acquaintance with the field, it

can by no means be termed "useful" because it is so tendentious. (See my attached report).

Reader's Report

Ammiel Alcalay's manuscript is highly problematic. There is certainly room for a new and fresh examination of the social, cultural and literary interaction between Jews and Arabs over historical time and geographical space. And indeed the literary aspects of this interaction (which seem to be this author's strong suit) are perhaps the least studied till now (except within certain discreet topical limits). Unfortunately, this manuscript fails to deliver. This is very much a piece of what might be called "popular French intellectual writing"; it never lets the facts get in the way of a good theory and it is enamored, even self-absorbed in its own rhetorical flourishes. The text is frequently couched in a dense, almost unreadable style, heavily salted with a few favorite catchwords which appear over and over again. "Space," "duration," and "memory" are prime examples of this. And of course, there is "palimpsest," which is often used metaphorically, although never literally. The pseudointellectual jargon is from time to time punctuated — rather jarringly — with popular and journalistic expressions (e.g., "x-ray vision") which is totally out of character with the purported tone. The manuscript is simply a total mishmash throughout. The first chapter tries to break out of the confines of the "rigid paradigms" of the historical disciplinary approach and moves back and forth from Maimonides to Osip Mandelstam, to Brenner, to the Description d'Egypte of Napoleon's scholars, to the *Guide Bleu* of the 1930s, to Edmond Jabès, and Tahar Benjelloun [sic]. Throughout these ramblings, the author makes all sorts of historical and political points that are never really developed, much less proven, but which really ought to be. Sometimes these points are taken up in the lengthy asides of the footnotes. Unfortunately, it is here that one sees the author's woefully inadequate knowledge of what has already been done in the field. He is frequently dependent upon highly unreliable secondary works, some of which are scarcely more than political tracts. Marion Woolfson's *Prophets in Babylon* is a case in point. Many of the gross generalizations regarding the lack of comprehensive studies on the multifaceted social relations "both within the Jewish communities and in relation to their societies" show appalling ignorance of the works of anthropologists such as Rosen, Geertz, Loeb, Deshen, Shokeid, Goldberg, and Bahloul, as well as historians, such as Zafrani in France, Ashtor and Hirschberg in Israel, Brown in England, Cohen, Schroeter, Stillman, Udovitch, and Valensi in the U.S.

The one major historian with whom the author is apparently familiar, and for whom he rightfully shows a great deal of admiration is S.D. Goitein. Chapter two, in fact, contains a very lengthy excursus on the Cairo Geniza and cites a potpourri of details from Goitein's magisterial work *A Mediterranean Society*. This section of the manuscript, however, does not gel very successfully with the rest of the text and should be excised. The author is clearly out of his depth here. If there is the embryo of a publishable book here, it is in the first and final chapters.

The author's strength is in describing how the Levant has been seen through 20th-century literary works, how Arabs and Jews viewed each other during the period of the rise of their respective nationalisms and in the period following the emergence of the State of Israel. Even here, however, there are some glaring weaknesses, for example, although the author is familiar with Israeli society during the 1950s and '60s, when Middle Easterners were at best ignored, and at worst suppressed, he is totally out of touch with Israeli society of the 1970s and '80s, when the situation changed dramatically and the Middle Eastern element began to be reclaimed and to assert itself both culturally and politically. (The author cannot retort that these decades are outside his highly idiosyncratic time limits — i.e., from the appearance of Dunash's wine song in ca. 965 to the Yemenite laments in 1951 — since he is never bothered by such temporal restrictions when it comes to airing his pet peeves).

What is most disturbing even in these stronger parts of the manuscript, is the thoroughly polemical tone and nature of the discourse. The author chooses only what fits his vision and conveniently ignores everything that does not. His one-sided depiction of the Arab in Israeli literature is a case in point. It fails to indicate that there was a range of attitudes from the romantic paternalism of Smilansky to the varied depictions in Yizhar, Shahar, Horgin, and others. Had he availed himself of other studies, such as G. Ramras-Rauch's *The Arab in Israeli Literature,* rather than mainly Fouzi El-Asmar's [sic] more partisan work, he might have presented an account of greater academic integrity. He might also have tried to give some sense of perspective by dealing with the image of Jews generally and Israeli [sic] particular[ly] in Arabic literature.

Sometimes in reading this manuscript, I was not sure whether it was out of ignorance or the narrowness of polemical vision that the author makes some of the statements that he does. He laments the fact that the texts of Hebrew writers of Arabic milieu are ignored, mentioning three examples: Burla, Shami, and Kahanoff. Of the three only Burla is a truly first rate littérateur, and it is simply false to say that he has been ignored. His novels are read in Israeli high schools and studied in universities in Israel, Europe and the United States. As for the other, they are really more mémoiristes, and even their work cannot be described as totally ignored. (There is in fact an interesting survey of these and other writers' recollections of their Islamicate backgrounds by Jacob Landau which the author has obviously not seen.) More contemporary writers of this milieu, such as Sami Michael and Amnon Shamosh[,] are not only widely read, but have had their works dramatized on Israeli television.

The author's hang ups so completely overwhelm the text at times as to make it ludicrous. Referring to the laureate of medieval Andalusian Jewry, Judah ha-Levi, he writes: "Yet like so many other works of the Levantine period these poems have been read less than used like the perennial elephant of the Jewish joke — to handily answer one of the many forms of the 'Jewish question,' as another piece of evidence fit into the mold of an already predetermined set of assumptions. At its most vulgar, Halevi is made into some kind of proto-Zionist; this metamorphosis, naturally, precludes emphasizing the fact that he was also known as Abu al-Hassan."

Speaking of vulgarity, the entire passage is crude, no less than it is false. The Arabic cultural formation of Judah ha-Levi is emphasized almost everywhere, whether in popular or scholarly writings. Passages such as this abound. They may score points with some people who have a political and cultural axe to grind (for example the readers of *Khamsin,* a polemical journal of dubious scholarship the author seems to read), but certainly not with any serious scholars. I fear that this book will do no better with the general educated reading public than with serious scholars. It is full of pseudo-intellectual jargon and bombast. For example, he states at the very outset that he is creating a model that "is ecological through the reclamation and recycling of antithetical episodes that can perforate circumscribed versions of history and serve to inform a forward looking future." That is sure to attract a general reader!

Polemical works can make very entertaining reading. They can be intellectually challenging. This ms., alas, is not in that category. It should not be published by a self-respecting academic press. It will, I am sure, eventually find a publisher among one of the small, politically-oriented presses in Paris or London.

There is, obviously, much that can be said about such a report and I proceeded to say it, as evident from the text that follows. Perhaps the only detail that I did not cover in my meticulous response was this writer's last point, that my manuscript would "eventually find a publisher among one of the small, politically-oriented presses in Paris or London." This was, in fact, a possibility I considered but it was very clear to me that such an option would even further neutralize the kinds of pressures I hoped the book could generate. The very terms in which this equation is stated point this out clearly: that is, the author of this report sees no contradiction or irony in encoding the word "political" to mean "not our politics," even as he or she is in the very process of excluding me from any access into that very political realm. At the risk of tedium, it seems to me that reproducing my response here in full serves diverse purposes that go beyond a merely documentary value; the title then used was not *After Jews and Arabs* but *Re:Orienting/Writing the Mediterranean*; in addition, the page numbers refer to the original, pre-publication manuscript:

> *Re:Orienting/Writing the Mediterranean* has primarily been an effort to shift the focus of a remarkably diverse literary and intellectual history (that of Jews and Arabs in the Near East) from the exclusive tutelage of an extremely narrow field of academic scholarship to the general community of literary scholars and students, from the traditional philological or "orientalist" approach to that of cultural studies and literary theory. In fact, this shift in literary focus has already occurred in other fields such as Asian studies, African and Afro-American studies, and Latin American studies, yet, as one of the reader's reports points out, "Middle Eastern studies has been, for the most part, remarkably absent from these debates." Unquestionably, any revisionist work is bound to meet some resistance along the way; my own awareness of this, along with the often heated emotional responses that the subject I have chosen to research sometimes elicits, made me all the more cautious regarding the scholarly and methodological foundations of my work. Given this, I sensed a definite bias towards my project in the second reader's report, a bias that, upon a close examination of the reader's objections, seems to rest more on an authority that would rather not be questioned or scrutinized than on intellectual rigor or scholarly evidence. Before surveying some of the particular inaccuracies contained in the report, a few general comments

seem in order. Throughout, the reader utilizes what might be termed a "hit and run" method, making a point without fully substantiating it. This, combined with an ad hominem critique only supported by tautological arguments that never get beyond judgmental and evaluative language to actually specify the reader's own contentions or position, all go into leaving the impression that this report is highly defensive but not very analytical. At the risk of being overly tedious, I would like to indulge in a point by point examination.

After summarizing the main goal of the work (in answer to question 1), the reader characterizes the evidence for my contentions as "highly selective, quite tendentious and often grossly misinterpreted." Yet, these claims are never fully substantiated in the body of the report. As far as selectivity goes, the reader states that I showed "appalling ignorance" of a number of anthropologists and historians; however, as I will document in detail further on, many of these figures are not only mentioned or cited but heavily relied on in my work. As far as being "tendentious" is concerned, the reader never states specifically what arguments are referred to nor why my work is generally characterized as "polemical." By then stating that I have "grossly misinterpreted" things, one can only come to the conclusion that this reader believes there is a correct and an incorrect interpretation to the very complex events, historical processes and texts that I present. This, in itself, is a highly suspect position in any academic context, and even more so in a field ("the social, cultural and literary interaction between Jews and Arabs over historical time and geographical space") in which the reader him/herself states that "there is certainly room for a new and fresh examination." "Indeed," the reader goes on to say, "the literary aspects of this interaction (which seem to be this author's strong suit) are perhaps the least studied till now." What is, perhaps, most puzzling about this report (a point that I will also go into further detail on when answering the objections to my second chapter), is that while the reader states that the "literary aspects" are my strength, these very literary aspects — as well as their conceptual and theoretical underpinnings — are all but ignored in the report. This, along with what appears to be an aversion to critical or literary theory, would lead me to believe that the reader's primary field of expertise is not literature; even were it a subsidiary field, the reader's language and terms of reference would seem to indicate that he/she is quite unfamiliar with and wholly outside the parameters of current debate, a debate that, I might add, has strongly influenced the practice of historical, anthropological and sociological writing, all fields that the reader emphasizes.

In answer to question 2, the reader states that "The author tries to disarm potential criticism by claiming to be an amateur." This is a reference to the second paragraph of my introduction: "*Re:Orienting / Writing the Mediterranean* is an amateur's attempt to shed some light on a realm that has been left in the hands of experts and ideologues too long." Given my range over literary, historical, theological, philosophical, sociological and anthropological works in over half a dozen languages, only a reader hard pressed to find fault would not see the irony involved in this introductory statement and not internally anticipate quotation marks over both "expert" and "amateur." Beyond even this more subtle point, I was surprised that the reader could not detect a reference to an article of mine from 1983 ("The Quill's Embroidery," *Parnassus: Poetry in Review*; Volume 11, Number 1; Spring/Summer 1983; pp. 85–115), an article that has come to be considered one of the most insightful introductions to Hebrew poetry written in English, where I discuss the late Professor Haim Schirmann's suggested mandatory equipment for the exegete of Hebrew poetry, a set of equipment that he almost comes to claim, tongue in cheek, impossible to acquire within one lifetime. Oddly enough, like the general lack of literary reference mentioned above, the reader barely mentions this primary concern and subject of the book, namely, Hebrew poetry. Further on in this same paragraph (in answer to question 2), the reader states that "He certainly has read a great deal, but he has also missed a great deal. Many of the false and exaggerated claims could not have been made if he had gone further." To begin with, and this is another point that will entail many specifics, the reader has read the manuscript quite selectively since many of the sources he claims I am ignorant of are, in fact, prominently cited. Moreover, these purportedly "false and exaggerated claims" are never specified. The certainty displayed here regarding truth and falsehood is, I daresay, a boundary I never overstep as examples I intend to quote on subjects I think the reader seems to be referring to will clearly indicate. Nor, for that matter, does the reader ever specify what makes this a "polemical" work rather than, as the first reader characterized it, a "radical critique, at once substantive and methodological, of a dominant version of the present sustained by a particular, and equally dominant, grasp on the materials of the past." Scholarly rigor notwithstanding, one had hoped that enough revisionist work has been done to make such claims to exclusivity a thing of the past. Yet, the reader continually characterizes the work judgmentally ("very much a piece of 'popular French intellectual writing' — it never lets the facts get in the way of a good theory"), without specifying the particulars: we are led to believe that there is, actually, only one set of facts (but can only assume which set since the reader never tells us), and, moreover, we are given to believe that my work rests on some grand "theory," rather than a continual questioning of assumptions along with a rigorous examination of both more traditional and neglected materials. Given some of the objections brought up in the body of the report, I would assume that the "false and exaggerated" claims the reader alludes to have to do with the relationship of Jews and Arabs as well as the transmission of the history and culture of Sephardi and Oriental Jews. This is substantiated by paragraph 2 on the second page of the report where the reader discusses my "one-sided depiction of the Arab in Israeli literature" as "a case in point." To begin with, the reader misrepresents my sources by saying that I relied mainly on the work of the Palestinian writer and critic Fawzi al-Asmar; in fact, all of the quotes I actually *used* in the section under scrutiny came from an Israeli critic, Ehud Ben-Ezer. In addition, I also cite the work of Risa Domb as well as Lev Hakak. Even given such a clear inaccuracy, this would not seem to me to be the point here. What appears to be at stake, in the reader's terms, is some sense of balance given to differing points of view and interpretations of the historical relationship between Jews and Arabs. Yet, even the most cursory (but unbiased) reading of my work shows that my statements are continually qualified and problematized; in fact, almost anywhere one turns, qualifications are made to particularize the general experience that I depict. Although the following examples are completely out of context, they should give some sense of what I mean.

Beginning with my introduction, I anticipate precisely the kind of objections that the reader seems to allude to without ever really specifying them: "Any attempt to "right" such volatile terrain, however, exposes one to accusations of righteousness, the replacement of one exclusivity for another. Setting something straight, of course, also presupposes that something's gone wrong, that once things were one way and now they're another. This, too, leaves the work open to a broadside, categorical critique in which the very structure of the work can be seen as a set up: once there was unity and harmony, now there is fragmentation and dissonance. Yet, the central categories that concern me — the qualities of mobility, diversity, autonomy and translatability possessed by the Jews of the Levant for a very long time — *have* eroded drastically. The marker for this, of course, is literal and unequivocal: most of the Jewish communities of the Mediterranean and Arab world simply no longer exist. Those that do are but a mere shadow of their former selves [...]. While I would obviously hold the qualities noted above as positive, they relate solely to themselves and do not necessarily imply further harmonies or idealized relations between either Arabs and Jews or Jews and themselves. The paradigms chosen to illustrate these qualities simply provide a catalog of possibilities that, given the constrictions of the present context, seem almost inconceivable [...]. *Re:Orienting* is not about victors and victims: to pit a powerless and gnawed at "East" against a voracious "West," with its consuming imagery, energy and capital, is to propose an argument as blind in its reliance on essences as the one it purportedly was trying to topple (pages iv–vi). As an aside, the reader objects to my "highly idiosyncratic time limits," again, completely out of context and conveniently ignoring my own very specific qualifications: "I have suggested a time span within whose limits (with befores and afters), a certain fluidity exists. This fluidity does not signal an ahistorical aversion to the specificities of time and place, but is an attempt (within a very broad framework), to mirror the conditions of space, at least as I have presented them, in the Levant. My sole justification for this is decidedly historical: Jews lived and traveled, settled down and created from one end of this realm to the other throughout the 1000-year period in question" (page vii).

But back to the main point of contention; by citing things out of context and choosing to emphasize certain aspects of my work while ignoring others, the reader leaves one with the impression that *Re:Orienting* is a grossly oversimplified, "one-sided" book. Again, quoting myself out of context, I would hope that a few examples can serve to give the general flavor of the kinds of qualifications I have been particularly careful to make in anticipation of just these kinds of objections. On page 21, in a discussion of some of the factors leading to the mass emigration/expulsion of Jews from Arab countries: "often, as in other periods throughout the history of the region, wealthier Jews could find themselves in a much better position than poor Muslims while the fate of poor Jews was often more closely linked to that of the Arab masses. Amongst Jews themselves, there were distinct divisions between the more culturally Arab working class (who lived in the traditional old Jewish Quarters, the *hara* or the *mellah*), and the more Europeanized middle and upper classes who tended to live in the newer quarters." Continuing on this topic (page 22), I go on to state that: "Here, the warring parties managed to find common ground. The increasingly reactionary Arab regimes also had their proverbial two birds and they, too, could be killed with one stone: by expelling the Jews, they could confiscate a substantial amount of wealth and property; at the same time, the Jewish question could be manipulated as a scapegoat to mask their own inert rhetoric, indifference and lack of resolve regarding the question of Palestine which, in turn, could help deflect attention from the more pressing, volatile and brutal power struggles and social conflicts transpiring in their own countries."

Again, out of context, the reader dwells on two issues, one of which has already been cited above: my "one-sided" depiction of "the image of the Arab in Israeli literature," as well as what I claim to be the neglect of "Hebrew writers of Arabic milieu." Just for the record, my discussion is not of "the image of the Arab in Israeli literature" but how a specific Hebrew novel that could not possibly be "Israeli," since it was written in the 1920s, sets one parameter of a fairly fixed set of characteristics. At any rate, on page 30, immediately after introducing these topics (pages 25–29), I take great care to specifically address the fact that ignorance of the "other" is not a one-sided phenomenon: "It is not only in Jerusalem that the number of people born into a new reality has multiplied: all over the Arab world (except in Morocco), there are fewer and fewer people who can still recall either the diverse Jewish cultural presence or the full range of human encounters with people who just happened to have been Jews; at the same time, there are more and more people for whom Jews can only be seen through the dull film of "Zionism," "Israel" and "war."

The discussion of the writers whose work I contend has been neglected is also taken completely out of the context in which I discuss it, that of being made into representatives of a particular kind within a subordinate culture by a dominant culture. In addition, there is a further inaccuracy regarding the work of the three writers in question which, though seemingly minor, just adds to the very generalized nature of the report. The reader "corrects" my categorization of them by stating that "Of the three only Burla is a truly first-rate littérateur. [...] As for the others, they are really mémoiristes." Disregarding the constant need to put things in a hierarchy, the fact is that Jaqueline Kahanoff wrote a novel and essays (in English, not Hebrew, as one might conclude from the report) as well as memoirs, while Shami only wrote novellas and short stories. Another example relating to my purported lack of balance can be found in the section on Beirut in chapter 1, where prominent attention is given to the detrimental effects certain ideological trends had on Arab culture; on page 67, "But unlike certain tenets of Arab nationalism which, like Zionism, attempted to reduce and homogenize a plethora of social, historical, economic, cultural, ethnic and religious differences under the all embracing rubric of either 'Arab' or 'Jew,' these writers expressed their vision of a borderless and uncensored Arabic as a way of speaking for people without a voice." By choosing to ignore my own often very critical discussions of events and texts emerging from the Arab world, the reader misrepresents my own sense of context and balanced argument entirely. Further examples of this abound, for instance: "Despite the short shrift given Muslims by the *Blue Guide,* during the 1,310-year period dating from the Arab conquest in 638 until 1948, there were only 129 years in which Jerusalem was not under one form or another of Islamic sovereignty. While this is not to suggest that such sovereignty was in any way uniform, ideal, or free from the practice of various kinds of occupation or exploitation" (page 94).

Again, in discussing the 1950's in Israel: "The implacable fate of the Jew writing Arabic in Israel was to remain unread: on one hand, the increasingly high and feverish pitch of official nationalist Arab culture cut off outside avenues of expression to anyone even remotely connected with 'the Zionist entity'; on the other hand, fewer and fewer Jews found the means to maintain the level of Arabic needed to contend with works of literature." Here, as I believe everywhere else, I try to point in at least two directions at the same time in order to do justice to the representation of incredibly complex phenomena.

In the second paragraph of page 1, the reader states that "The manuscript is simply a total mishmash throughout." There follows a list of a number of authors, again taken completely out of context and without supporting evidence, that is supposed to serve as final proof for an argument the reader has not yet fully or even partially clarified. The seeming disparity of the authors is made an end in itself ("from Maimonides to Osip Mandelstam, to Brenner"), as if such a range already presupposed some kind of incoherence. Almost at random, I chose a book to see what range of authors or sources might be quoted or referred to within the space, not even of a chapter, but a few pages. The book, *On the Art of Medieval Arabic Literature* by Prof. Andras Hamori of Princeton University, is considered one of, if not *the* finest exposition on Arabic literature currently available. In the words of the great scholar Franz Rosenthal: "Professor Hamori's book is distinguished by the fact that it attempts to take Arabic literature, mainly poetry, seriously and to apply the canons of modern literary criticism to it. There are hardly any books in English comparable to it, and few in other European languages." In a discussion of a certain genre of Arabic poetry, Hamori mentions Spenser, Ariosto, Homer, the Serbo-Croatian epic and Heidegger in the space of two pages (74–75). Again, in a discussion of pre-Islamic Arabic poetry, Hamori mentions R.P. Blackmur, *The Death of Arthur*, Chaucer's *Troilus*, Plato, Socrates, Homer and Chinese poetry of the "Double Ninth Festival," all in the space of three pages (20–22). Does the mention of these things together immediately connote incoherence? Possibly, but certainly not in the specific context that Hamori has chosen to use them.

The reader then goes on to write that "Throughout these ramblings the author makes all sorts of historical and political points [...]. Sometimes these points are taken up in the lengthy asides of the footnotes. Unfortunately, it is here that one sees the author's woefully inadequate knowledge of what has already been done in the field." Despite my painstaking and, as I stated earlier, possibly tedious examination of the report, it is only at this point that the reader's bias, through the obvious contradictions engendered by selective reading, becomes clear. After having given the impression that he has read the text and the footnotes thoroughly, the reader states that "He is frequently dependent upon highly unreliable secondary works, some of which are scarcely more than political tracts. Marion Woolfson's *Prophets in Babylon* is a case in point." Entirely skipping the very valid question of just what constitutes either a "highly unreliable" source or a "political tract," the reader has chosen to mention a work that I referred to only once in a footnote (Chapter 1, footnote 11, p. 107). The report then goes on to state that I show "appalling ignorance" of a number of anthropologists and historians. Oddly enough, I mention many of these figures more prominently than I do Woolfson. The work of one of the anthropologists that I am purportedly appallingly ignorant of, in fact, is used to form a significant part of my argument in two chapters (the anthropologist in question is Harvey Goldberg; see chapter 2, pages 132–135; also see chapter 3, pages 262–264, particularly footnotes 14 and 16, pages 288–289). While the passages mentioned in the text heavily rely on Goldberg, in footnote 14, I state that Goldberg's "whole introduction is well worth referring to as an example of a highly sensitive reading of completely forgotten material." Another example is the case of the great historian Elihayu Ashtor, someone who also appears on the reader's list. Yet, in the footnotes to chapter 2, he is mentioned twice: footnote 3, page 240 and footnote 5, page 240, where I call his *The Jews of Moslem Spain* (in 3 volumes), "the standard work on the 'golden age' of the Jews during this period." Not to know this, of course, would truly be an appalling indictment of one's lack of knowledge in the field. There are other examples, as well: Shlomo Deshen, an anthropologist, is mentioned on page 109, in footnote 18 to chapter 1. Clifford Geertz, Joelle Bahloul, Haim Zafrani, Norman Stillman and H.Z. Hirschberg all figure prominently in my bibliography. On page 3 of his report, the reader mentions an article by Jacob Landau "which the author has obviously not seen." The tone of assurance is even more striking here given the fact that on page 242, in footnote 29 to chapter 2, I specifically refer to the article in question: "For a survey of some examples of this genre of memoir, see Jacob M. Landau's 'Bittersweet Nostalgia: Memoirs of Jewish Immigrants from the Arab Countries.'" Right after this, the reader mentions two contemporary Israeli authors whom I am also apparently unaware of, Sami Michael and Amnon Shamosh. Michael is discussed on pages 303–304, where I note that he has become a significant writer on the contemporary Israeli scene. The works of Shamosh are also mentioned in the bibliography; what any of this has to do with dramatization on Israeli television is well beyond my grasp.

Yet, even more disturbing than these blatant inaccuracies are the assumptions and inferences drawn from such a selective reading. The fact that the reader is careful enough to point out that a publication date is missing in a footnote or that a quotation goes over from one page to another (noted with an exclamation point), while assuming I am ignorant of scholars, writers and articles that I mention prominently, can only lead one to conclude that some form of bias is at work here. An example of this can be seen on page 3 where the reader has taken a quote completely out of context in order to make another point that is, again, left unsubstantiated: "The Arabic cultural formation of Judah ha-Levi is emphasized almost everywhere, whether in popular or scholarly writings. Passages such as this abound. They may score points with some people who have a political and cultural axe to grind (for example the readers of *Khamsin,* a polemical journal of dubious scholarship the author seems to read), but not with any serious scholars." What kind of an axe? Which serious scholars? Which popular or scholarly writings? None of this is specified, nor is the innocent receiver of this report at any time given a fair representation of the range of sources that I did consult and that I am familiar with. In fact, this kind of argument is a gross misrepresentation of the range of my own scholarship for the huge areas it simply neglects to mention. For, as a reader of the journal *Khamsin,* I am also the reader of *The Hebrew Union College Annual, Jewish Quarterly Review, Revue des études juives, Encyclopedia of Islam, Encyclopedia Judaica, The Jewish Encyclopedia,* and numerous other standard sources. Why is *Khamsin* singled out (although only two issues are cited throughout), when other standard sources that are referred to more often are never mentioned? And why is the context of the quote, which has to do with the way cultures are transmitted by dominant groups and ideologies for particular purposes, never mentioned?

There are many other questionable aspects: in the second paragraph on page 2, the reader states that "although the author is familiar with Israeli society during the 1950s and '60s, when Middle Easterners were at best ignored, and at worst suppressed, he is totally out of touch with Israeli society of the 1970s and 1980s, when the situation changed dramatically and the Middle Eastern element began to be reclaimed and to assert itself both culturally and politically. (The author cannot retort that these decades are outside his highly idiosyncratic time limits...)." Here, the reader simply seems to have conveniently skipped the last sections of the last chapter which specifically address the late 1970s and 1980s (see pages 305–329). Moreover, a recent article of mine ("Israel and the Levant: "Wounded Kinship's Last Resort"), provides one of the most thorough surveys of "Oriental" Israeli culture in the 1980s to appear in English, not to mention my socio-political study (published in 1987) on political attitudes of Jews from Arab countries which has become a standard in the field ("La communaute sepharade en Israel et le processus de paix," *Perspectives Judeo-Arabes*; No. 7; August, 1987; pp. 47–85).

An even larger issue that must be addressed here has to do with the question of literature itself. It is certainly odd that while the reader acknowledges the "literary aspects" of the field to be my strength, chapter 2 of the book (which deals extensively with Hebrew poetry and Jewish literature as well as the relationship of Hebrew and Arabic poetics to literature in the romance languages), "does not gel very successfully with the rest of the text and should be excised. The author is clearly out of his depth here." This seems like a major contradiction, yet, again, no evidence is given as to why I am "out of my depth;" it is simply stated as fact and linked to my use of the work of S.D. Goitein, "The one major historian with whom the author is apparently familiar." This kind of disparaging remark is nowhere warranted by the range of sources that are used even within the particular section where Goitein is used as a primary source (only 24 pages of a 130 page chapter). Some of the sources in the historical section of the chapter (comprising 40 pages, including the Goitein section), include: Eliyahu Ashtor (mentioned earlier), Walter J. Fischel (a pioneer in studying the economic and political life of Jews in medieval Islam), Oleg Grabar (the foremost historian of Islamic art), Muhsin Mahdi and Ralph Lerner (two of the most respected authorities on medieval political philosophy), Jacob Mann (another pioneer in geniza studies, and a standard in the field), Jacob Landau (mentioned earlier), and Harvey Goldberg (mentioned earlier). This is just a partial listing and does not even begin to mention the range of sources consulted (and included on the bibliography), but not cited. These include many standard sources such as Salo Baron's classic *A Political and Religious History of the Jews* (12 volumes); Itshak Baer's *History of the Jews in Christian Spain*; the work of Fernand Braudel on the Mediterranean; Andre Chouraqui's work on North African Jewry; Norman Daniel's indispensable studies on the relationship of Islam and the West; Bayard Dodge's standard work on medieval Muslim education; Renzo DeFelice's work on the Jews of Libya; the extremely important but often neglected works of Levantine Jewish historians like Abraham Galante, Moise Franco, Joseph Toledano, Michael Molho and Joseph Nehama; the classic orientalist works of Ignaz Goldziher; Marshall Hodgson's monumental *The Venture of Islam*; the work of Philip K. Hitti and Albert Hourani; Reuben Levy's classic *The Social Struc-*

ture of Islam; the works of Bernard Lewis and Maxime Rodinson; Andre Raymond and Janet Abu-Lughod's important works on Arab cities; Norman Stillman (mentioned earlier); the works of Georges Vajda, Moise Ventura, Harry Wolfson, Zvi Werblowsky and Gershom Scholem on Jewish philosophy and mysticism; and Yosef Yerushalmi's important work on Sephardi and Marrano Jews, to mention only some.

Not to even mention the range of sources I bring to bear on the major part of chapter 2, that is, the literary part, seems, at best, disingenuous. My own qualifications in the field are not without distinction: I had both the luck and honor to be a student of the late Dan Pagis for a number of years when I was at the Hebrew University in Jerusalem. Pagis brought the study of medieval, renaissance and post-expulsion Hebrew poetry into the modern age through his groundbreaking works, *Secular Poetry and Poetic Theory: Moses Ibn Ezra and His Contemporaries* and *Change and Tradition in Secular Poetry: Spain and Italy*. Through studying with Pagis at Hebrew University, I passed the standard apprenticeship of those drawn, or better yet, magnetized to classical Andalusian Hebrew poetry. This meant a thorough knowledge of the standard works by scholars like Haim Brody, David Yellin, Shimon Bernstein, Ezra Fleischer, Yehuda Ratzaby, Haim Schirmann, Nehemia Allony, Shaul Abdullah Yosef, Dov Yarden and Ben Zion Halper, as well as keeping abreast of the latest developments in Israeli, Spanish and Anglo-American scholarship, the three major sites of research. All of these sources are generously referred to in chapter 2 of *Re:Orienting*. Nor is this all: in addition to covering the classical period in Andalusia, there is an extensive discussion of Arabic poetics and its relation to both Hebrew poetry as well as the development of the romance lyric. Having been a student of both Allen Mandelbaum and Frederick Goldin, my sources here, as well (in Italian, Spanish, French and Provencal), meet all the standards. The chapter closes with a completely original piece of research on a Marrano poet who translated Petrarch in 1567; this is followed by an extensive discussion on the extant poetry of Jewish women in the Levant and how some recognition of these works might change many of our assumptions about the whole period. Yet, the reader's report mentions none of this, despite the contention that the "literary aspects" remain my "strong suit."

Finally, throughout the report, the reader criticizes my writing through labels, not analysis; some of these epithets include "dense style and bombast; almost unreadable style, heavily salted with a few favorite catchwords; pseudo-intellectual jargon." There are others, as well, but they never seem to fully explain what the reader's objections actually consist of. Here is a case in point: the reader states that the few favorite catchwords are "space," "duration," and "memory." These are simply brought up as final proof of the reader's argument without any legitimate grounds for discounting the use of these particular words. Again: "The pseudo-intellectual jargon is from time to time punctuated — rather jarringly — with popular and journalistic expressions (e.g. "x-ray vision") which is totally out of character with the purported tone." This is very difficult to grasp since the reader never specifies what my "purported tone" is supposed to be, nor is this made any clearer by the reader's own characterization of my writing. In addition, all of the quotes, phrases and even single words are taken completely out of context. It is quite interesting to note that this reader chose precisely the same sentence (as a primary example of "pseudo intellectual jargon and bombast") that the first reader chose as an "apt description" of my methodology. Not to blow my own trumpet, but that the quality of my writing should be attacked is, indeed, the oddest part of this report as I hope some of the following quotes might illustrate. Outside of the praise that one is always flattered to get, particularly from established figures whose work has been so essential to my own development, the important point about these quotes is the fact that they come from scholars and writers for whom writing itself, and style, are not, by any means, negligible qualities.

"Ammiel Alcalay is that rare thing — a gifted prose writer and poet, an accomplished intellectual and a true, as well as inventive, comparatist."

Edward Said,
Old Dominion Foundation Professor in the Humanities,
Columbia University

"It is rare that someone has both an articulately perceptive grasp of cultural and political particulars and an art capable of their transmission in all the determining context of their fact. Ammiel Alcalay is far more than the usual cultural historian, or political scientist, or, simply, scholar of complexly "comparative literature."

Robert Creeley,
SUNY Distinguished Professor,
Samuel P. Capen Professor of Poetry and the Humanities;
member, American Academy and
Institute of Arts and Letters

"As an accomplished poet, social commentator and historical investigator, as well as a tireless researcher, Ammiel Alcalay has pulled together many of the strands gathered during years of prodigious scholarship to present a view of the Middle East that is starkly at odds with that put forth in the establishment press and academic journals. Painstakingly, brick by brick, he has reconstructed a shared literary and historical tradition that has linked Arab and Oriental Jewish thought for the better part of milennium."

Victor Perera, Lecturer, Journalism and Spanish Literature,
University of California, Santa Cruz

"Since the early 1980s I have been following the cultural involvements of Ammiel Alcalay with exceeding interest and admiration [...]. His translations of Hanagid and Halevi (among others), reflected, in the most intricate manner, his loyalties and appetites. However, in retrospect, this seems a mere honing of the tools for the main project that Alcalay took upon himself in recent years. I followed closely the writing of his *Re:Orienting / Writing the Mediterranean,* not only because I was a subject of scrutiny, but, mainly, because of the extreme relevance of this pioneering study to the current cultural scene of the Middle East. His reading of that turbulent region ranks among the most creative and imaginative readings of history that I, being so obsessed with the same subject matter, have ever come across."

Anton Shammas, Visiting Lecturer,
University of Michigan at Ann Arbor

"I am impressed by the breadth of his knowledge, his uncompromising lucidity, and his commitment to the Mediterranean — a region too often maligned, idealized, or ignored. Alcalay's scholarly and creative production is, especially for a comparatist of his age, astounding [...]. Alcalay's writing is superb. The activity of reading — or remembering a history — becomes in these pages nothing less than a quest for knowledge. The reader is jolted out of the comforts of received polemic, as Alcalay questions our conventional ways of thinking not only about the Middle East, but about Western civilization and European culture."

[Colin] Joan Dayan, Chair,
Department of Comparative Literature, Queens College;
1990 Fellow, Shelby Collum Davis Center for Historical Study

Along with my response, quoted in full above, I sent the following letter, dated March 1st, 1990:

Enclosed is my rather lengthy rejoinder to the second reader's report on *Re:Orienting.* I really wanted to make sure that nothing got by on this so it took me little longer than I thought it would.

It may simply be that I've gotten used to this kind of a reaction to my work from certain quarters, but only after thoroughly examining this report against my own work did I truly realize just how vicious and personal an attack this particular one actually is. I've run my reply by a number of people and I don't think that it should in any way be offensive to anyone — I've kept quite strictly to the specifics of the arguments involved. However, you obviously know your editorial board better than I do and I'd appreciate if you went over it and let me know if you think there's anything there that might rub someone the wrong way. I think, though, that this reply utterly demolishes the reader's credibility and exposes the kinds of bias involved.

As an aside (and I wouldn't in any way want this to interfere with the editorial process nor do I know whether this is standard procedure or not), I think it might prove a valuable exercise for the reader to see my reply, if for nothing else at least to know that not everyone is willing to be bullied and cowed into silence by "authority." Nor would I want this to be construed as some kind of vengeance on my part. I just became more and more amazed at the audacity (dare I say *men*dacity) of the reader's claims as I examined them point by point. Disagreement is one thing, academic arguments with proof are another, but selective reading and willful misrepresentation simply have no place in this kind of a process.

The appeal failed and the book continued to circulate until it came out, as I mentioned, in 1993; although it was named one of the twenty-five notable books of the year by the *Village Voice Literary Supplement* and one of the year's choices by the *Independent* in London, the book was generally ignored in academic and mainstream venues where the work of its "anonymous" critics regularly appeared. On the other hand, *After Jews and Arabs* has had an influence disproportionate to its circulation: like the method of poetry, those who read it have paid attention, with the idea of using the information it contains for their own purposes. The book has also forced Israeli literary scholars to reconsider some of their assumptions, while engendering a concerted effort among *mizrahi* writers, scholars, and activists to publish standardized editions and anthologies of neglected or forgotten writers that can be used as textbooks. At the same time, it has opened a window onto a very neglected aspect of Jewish culture within the Arab world — while there are numerous indications of this, a formal and symbolic marker was an invitation that I received to participate in a conference commemorating the fiftieth anniversary of the Nakba, the disaster of 1948, held in Beirut. Unlike the kinds of invitations that I was getting after the Oslo Accords, this one carried profound meaning for me.

3

Bibliography for Ammiel Alcalay, *After Jews & Arabs: Remaking Levantine Culture* (Minneapolis: University of Minnesota Press, 1993)

Completed in 1992

I. Sources: Anthologies and Collections

Alvar, Manuel, ed. *Poesía Tradicional de los Judíos Españoles.* Mexico: Editorial Porrua, 1966.

Arkin, Marian, and Barbara Shollar, eds. *Longman Anthology of World Literature by Women, 1875–1975.* New York: Longman, 1989.

Badran, Margot, and Miriam Cooke, eds. *Opening the Gates: A Century of Arab Feminist Writing.* Bloomington: Indiana University Press, 1990.

Benson, Peter, ed. "Recent African Writing: New Forms, Old Forms, New Themes, Old Themes." *The Literary Review* 34, no. 4 (Summer 1991).

Benson, Thomas W., and Michael H. Prosser, eds. *Readings in Classical Rhetoric.* Bloomington: Indiana University Press, 1972.

Bernstein, Shimon, ed. *Hebrew Poetry from Italy.* Jerusalem, 1939. [Hebrew]

Besso, Henry V. *Dramatic Literature of the Sephardic Jews of Amsterdam in the XVIIth and XVIIIth Centuries.* New York: Hispanic Institute in the U.S., Sección De Estudios Sefardíes, 1947.

Bezirgan, Basima Qattan, and Elizabeth Warnock Fernea, eds. *Middle Eastern Muslim Women Speak.* Austin: University of Texas Press, 1977.

Blackburn, Paul, trans. *Proensa: An Anthology of Troubadour Poetry.* Edited by George Economou. Berkeley: University of California Press, 1978.

Bogin, Meg. *The Women Troubadours.* New York: Paddington, 1976.

Booth, Marilyn, trans. *My Grandmother's Cactus: Stories by Egyptian Women.* London: Quartet, 1991.

Boullata, Issa J., ed. and trans. *Modern Arab Poets: 1950–1975.* Washington, DC: Three Continents, 1976.

Boullata, Kamal, ed. and trans. *Women of the Fertile Crescent: An Anthology of Modern Poetry by Arab Women.* Washington, DC: Three Continents, 1981.

Brennan, Tim, ed. "Writing from Black Britain." *The Literary Review* 34, no. 1 (Fall 1990): 5–11.

Bushnaq, Inea, ed. *Arab Folktales.* New York: Pantheon, 1986.

Campbell, Joseph, ed. *The Portable Arabian Nights.* Translated by John Payne. New York: Viking, 1952.

Cantarino, Vincente, ed. *Arabic Poetics in the Golden Age: Selection of Texts Accompanied by a Preliminary Study.* Leiden: E.J. Brill, 1975.

Carmi, T., ed. *The Penguin Book of Hebrew Verse.* New York: Viking, 1981.

Caspi, Mishael Maswari. *Daughters of Yemen.* Berkeley: University of California Press, 1985.

Chan, Jeffery Paul, Frank Chin, Lawson Fusao Inada, and Shawn Wong, eds. *The Big Aiiieeeee! An Anthology of Chinese American and Japanese American Literature.* New York: Meridian, 1991.

Dan, Joseph, ed. *The Early Kabbalah.* Translated by Ronald C. Kiener. New York: Paulist Press, 1986.

Doria, Charles, and Harris Lenowitz, eds. *Origins: Creation Texts from the Ancient Mediterranean.* Garden City: Anchor, 1976.

Fine, Lawrence, trans. *Safed Spirituality: Rules of Mystical Piety, the Beginning of Wisdom.* New York: Paulist Press, 1984.

Freehof, Solomon Bennett, ed. *The Responsa Literature and A Treasury of Responsa.* New York: KTAV, 1973.

Gabrieli, Francesco, ed. and trans. (from Arabic sources). *Arabic Histories of the Crusades.* Translated by E.J. Costello (from Italian sources). London: Routledge and Kegan Paul, 1969.

Goitein, S.D., trans. *Letters of Medieval Jewish Traders.* Princeton: Princeton University Press, 1973.

Goldin, Frederick. *German and Italian Lyrics of the Middle Ages.* Garden City: Anchor, 1973.

———. *Lyrics of the Troubadours and Trouvères: An Anthology and a History.* Garden City: Anchor, 1973.

Goldstein, David. *The Jewish Poets of Spain, 900–1250.* Harmondsworth: Penguin, 1971.

Goméz, Emilio García. *Poemas Arábigoandaluces.* Madrid: Editorial Plutarco, 1930.

———. *Cinco Poetas Musulmanes.* Madrid: Espasa-Calpe, 1945.

Gottheil, Richard, and William H. Worrell, eds. *Fragments from the Cairo Geniza in the Freer Collection.* New York: MacMillan, 1927.

Halper, Ben Zion. *Post Biblical Hebrew Literature: An Anthology.* Philadelphia: The Jewish Publication Society of America, 1921.

Hamalian, Leo, and John D. Yohannan, eds. *New Writing from the Middle East.* New York: New American Library, 1978.

Harshav, Benjamin, and Barbara Harshav. *American Yiddish Poetry: A Bilingual Anthology.* Berkeley: University of California Press, 1986.

Hayyim, Yosef. *Mahzor Tefilat Yesharim haShalem le-Yom Kippur.* Jerusalem: Saleh Mansour, 1981. [Hebrew]

Hutchins, William M., ed. *Egyptian Tales and Short Stories of the 1970s and 1980s.* Cairo: The American University in Cairo Press, 1987.
Jayyusi, Salma Khadra, ed. *Modern Arabic Poetry: An Anthology.* New York: Columbia University Press, 1987.
———. *Literature of Modern Arabia.* London: Kegan Paul, 1988.
Johnson-Davies, Denys, trans. *Arabic Short Stories.* London and New York: Quartet, 1983.
Khouri, Mounah A., and Hamid Algar, eds. *An Anthology of Modern Arabic Poetry.* Berkeley: University of California Press, 1974.
Kobler, Franz, ed. *Letters of Jews through the Ages.* 2 vols. New York: Hebrew Publishing Company, 1978.
Kritzeck, James. *Anthology of Islamic Literature.* New York: Mentor Book by New American Library, 1966.
Lelchuk, Allen, and Gershon Shaked, eds. *Eight Great Hebrew Short Novels.* New York: Meridian, 1983.
Leviant, Curt, ed. *Masterpieces of Hebrew Literature.* New York: KTAV, 1969.
Lichtenstadter, Ilse. *Introduction to Classical Arabic Literature.* New York: Schocken, 1976.
Lyall, Charles James. *Translations of Ancient Arabian Poetry: Chiefly Pre-Islamic.* New York: Columbia University Press, 1930.
Macey, Jeffrey, ed. *Readings in Medieval Jewish and Islamic Philosophy.* Jerusalem: Hebrew University Press, 1979.
Mahdi, Muhsin, and Ralph Lerner, eds. *Medieval Political Philosophy: A Sourcebook.* New York: The Free Press, 1963.
Makarius, Raoul, and Laura Makarius, eds. *Anthologie de la littérature arabe contemporaine.* 3 vols. Paris: Éditions de Seuil, 1964.
Mann, Jacob. *Texts and Studies in Jewish Literature.* New York: KTAV, 1972.
Manzalaoui, Mahmoud, ed. *Arabic Short Stories.* Cairo: The American University in Cairo Press, 1985.

Marcus, J.R. *The Jew in the Medieval World: A Sourcebook, 315–1791.* New York: Atheneum, 1974.

Memmi, Albert, ed. *Anthologie des écrivains maghrébins d'expression française.* Paris: Présence Africaine, 1965.

Misrahi, Hanina. *The History of Persian Jews and their Poets.* Jerusalem: Rubin Mass, 1966. [Hebrew]

Monroe, James T. *Hispano-Arabic Poetry: A Student Anthology.* Berkeley: University of California Press, 1974.

Moreh Shmuel, ed. *Short Stories by Jewish Writers from Iraq.* Jerusalem: Magnes Press, 1982. [Arabic and Hebrew]

Muhawi, Ibrahim, and Sharif Kanaana. *Speak Bird, Speak Again: Palestinian Arab Folktales.* Berkeley: University of California Press, 1989.

Neubauer, Adolf, ed. *Medieval Jewish Chronicles and Chronological Notes.* 2 vols. Oxford: Oxford University Press, 1887–1895.

Oelman, Timothy, ed. *Marrano Poets of the 17th Century.* Rutherford: Farleigh Dickinson University Press, 1982.

Pagis, Dan. *Like a Scarlet Thread: Hebrew Love Poetry from Spain, Italy, Turkey, and the Yemen.* Tel Aviv: Hakibbutz Hameuchad, 1979. [Hebrew]

Phillips, J.J., Ishmael Reed, Gundars Strads, and Shawn Wong, eds. *The Before Columbus Foundation Poetry Anthology.* New York: W.W. Norton, 1992.

Ratzaby, Yehuda, ed. *An Anthology of the Hebrew Maqam.* Jerusalem: Bialik Institute, 1974. [Hebrew]

Reed, Ishmael, Kathryn Trueblood, and Shawn Wong, eds. *The Before Columbus Foundation Fiction Anthology.* New York: W.W. Norton, 1992.

Rothenberg, Jerome, ed. *Technicians of the Sacred: A Range of Poetries from Africa, America, Asia, Europe & Oceania.* Berkeley: University of California Press, 1985.

Rothenberg, Jerome, Harris Lenowitz, and Charles Doria, eds. *A Big Jewish Book.* Garden City: Anchor Doubleday, 1978.

Sadeh, Pinhas. *Jewish Folktales.* New York: Anchor, 1989.

Scheindlin, Raymond P. *Wine, Women and Death: Medieval Hebrew Poems on the Good Life*. Philadelphia: The Jewish Publication Society of America, 1986.

———. *The Gazelle: Medieval Hebrew Poems on God, Israel and the Soul*. Philadelphia: Jewish Publication Society of America, 1991.

Schirmann, Haim, ed. *Anthology of Hebrew Poetry in Italy*. Berlin: Shoken, 1934. [Hebrew]

———, ed. *Hebrew Poetry in Spain and Provence*. 4 vols. Jerusalem: Bialik Insitute, 1956. [Hebrew]

Seder Arba'a Ta'aniyot ke-Minhag Sefarad [Order of the Four Fasts According to the Sephardic Rite]. Tel Aviv: Sinai, 1977. [Hebrew]

Sefer Shirei Yedidot [Liturgical Poetry of Moroccan Jews]. Jerusalem: Yosef Lugassi, 1979. [Hebrew]

Shir u'Shebacha, Hallel v'Zimra [Liturgical Poetry of Syrian Jews]. New York: Magen David, 1983. [Hebrew]

Shoshannah, Rabbi Hayyim Raphael. *E'ira Shahar* [Liturgical Poetry of Moroccan Jews]. Beersheva: Hotsa'at Nitzanim, 1979. [Hebrew]

Stern, S.M. *Les Chanson Mozarabes*. Palermo: Università di Palermo, 1953.

———. "Arabic Poems by Spanish Hebrew Poets." In *Romanica et Occidentalia: Études dédiées à la Mémoire de Hiram Peri*, ed. Moshe Lazar, 254–63. Jerusalem: Magnes Press, 1963.

———. *Hispano-Arabic Strophic Poetry*. Edited by L.P. Harvey. Oxford: Clarendon, 1974.

Trypanis, C.A. *The Penguin Book of Greek Verse*. Harmondsworth: Penguin, 1971.

Tuetey, Charles Greville, ed. *Classical Arabic Poetry: 162 Poems from Imrulkais to Maari*. London: Routledge and Kegan Paul, 1985.

Udhari al, Abdallah. *Victims of a Map*. London: Al Saqi, 1984.

———. *Modern Poetry of the Arab World*. New York: Penguin, 1986.

Udhari al, Abdallah, and G.B.H. Wightman, eds. *Birds Through a Ceiling of Alabaster: Three Abbasid Poets*. Harmondsworth: Penguin, 1975.
Washington, Mary Helen, ed. *Invented Lives*. New York: Anchor, 1987.
———. *Black-Eyed Susans, Midnight Birds*. New York: Anchor, 1990.
———. *Memory of Kin*. New York: Anchor, 1991.
Williams, John Alden. *Themes of Islamic Civilization*. Berkeley: University of California Press, 1982.

II. Premodern Sources: Single Authors

Abranavel, Judah. *The Philosophy of Love*. Edited by F. Friedberg Seeley and J.H. Barnes. London: Soncino, 1937.
Abulafia, Todros. *Gan ha'Meshalim v'haHidot: The Garden of Apologues and Saws: Being the Diwan of Don Todros Halevi en Abu-Alafiah*. Edited with notes and commentary by David Yellin. 4 vols. London: 1926; Jerusalem: 1932–1936. [Hebrew]
Alemán, Mateo. *Guzmán de Alfarache*. 2 vols. Madrid: Escolar, 1977.
Almoli, Shlomo. *The Interpretation of Dreams*. Constantinople, 1530. [Hebrew]
Almosnino, Moses. *Extremos y Grandezas de Constantinople*. Translated by Jacob Cansino. Madrid: F. Martinez, 1638.
———. *Transformaciones de Morpheo: o Tractado de Sueños*. Amsterdam, 1734.
Ascarelli, Devora. *Sindicato Italiani Arti*. Rome: Pellegrino Ascarelli, 1925.
Asséns, Raphael Cansinos-Asséns, trans. *El Korán*. Madrid: Aguilar, 1963.
———, trans. *Libro de las Mil y Una Noches*. 3 vols. Madrid: Aguilar, 1969.
Bar Hayya, Abraham. *The Meditation of a Sad Soul*. Edited and translated by Geoffrey Wigoder. New York: Schocken, 1968.

Benjamin of Tudela. *The Itinerary of Benjamin of Tudela.* Critical text, translation, and commentary by Marcus Nathan Adler. Henry Frowde: London, 1907.

Ben Labrat, Dunash. *Poems.* Edited by Nehemia Allony. Jerusalem: Mossad haRav Kook, 1947. [Hebrew]

Blecua, Alberto, ed. *Lazarillo de Tormes.* Madrid: Castalia, 1979.

Cardozo, Isaac. *Las Excelencias y Calumnias de los Hebreos.* Amsterdam, 1679.

Cervantes, Miguel de. *Don Quixote.* Translated by J.M. Cohen. Harmondsworth: Penguin, 1950.

Chaucer, Geoffrey. *Complete Works.* Edited by W.W. Skeat. London: Oxford, 1912.

DaPiera, Shlomo ben Meshullam. *Diwan.* Edited by S. Bernstein. 2 vols. New York, 1942–1946. [Hebrew]

De La Vega, Joseph Penso. *Confusion de Confusiones.* Amsterdam, 1688.

———. *Confusion de Confusiones.* Translated by Hermann Kellenbenz. Boston: Baker Library, 1957.

Delicado, Francesco. *La lozána andaluza.* Madrid: Castalia, 1969.

Garmon, Rabbi Nehorai. *Rabbi Nehorai Garmon of Tunisia and His Poetry.* Edited by Michal Saraf. Tel Aviv: Tel Aviv University Press, 1982. [Hebrew]

HaCohen, Joseph. *'Emeq haBekha.* Edited by Meir Wiener. Leipzig: Oskar Leiner, 1858. [Hebrew]

HaKohen, Mordekhai. *The Book of Mordekhai.* Edited by Harvey Goldberg. Philadelphia: Institute for the Study of Human Issues, 1980.

Halevi, Yehuda. *Diwan.* Edited by Haim Brody. 4 vols. Berlin, 1894–1930. [Hebrew]

———. *Selected Poems.* Translated by Nina Salaman. Philadelphia: The Jewish Publication Society of America, 1924.

———. *Zveiundneunzig Hymen und Gedichte.* Translated by Franz Rosenzweig. Berlin: Verlag Lambert Schneider, 1927.

———. *The Liturgical Poetry of Yehdua haLevi.* Edited by Dov Yarden. 4 vols. Dov Yarden: Jerusalem, 1978–1985. [Hebrew]

HaNakdan, Berachia. *Fables of a Jewish Aesop*. Translated by Moshe Hadas. New York: Columbia University Press, 1967.

Hariri, al-Qasim ibn Ali. *The Assemblies of al-Hariri*. Translated by Thomas Chenery. Edinburgh, 1867.

———. *Machberot Ithiel*. Edited by Yitshak Perets and translated by Yehuda al-Harizi. Tel Aviv: Mosad ha-Rav Kuk, 1955. [Hebrew]

Harizi, Yehuda al-. *Sefer Tahkemoni*. Edited by J. Toporovsky. Tel Aviv: Mosad ha-Rav Kuk, 1952. [Hebrew]

———. *The Tahkemoni*. Translated by Victor Emanuel Reichert. 2 vols. Jerusalem: Raphal Haim Cohen, 1965–1973.

Ibn al-Arabi. *The Bezels of Wisdom*. Translated by R.W.J. Austin. New York: Paulist Press, 1980.

Ibn Altabban, Levi. *Poems*. Edited by Dan Pagis. Jerusalem: The Israeli Academy of Sciences and Humanities, 1967. [Hebrew]

Ibn Ezra, Abraham. *Essays on the Writings of Ibn Ezra*. Edited by M. Friedlander. London: Trübner for the Society of Hebrew Literature 1877.

———. *Ibn Ezra on Isaiah*. Edited by M. Friedlander. London: Trübner for the Society of Hebrew Literature, 1877. [Hebrew]

———. *Religious Poems*. Edited by I. Levin. Jerusalem: The Israeli Academy of Sciences and Humanities, 1975–1980. [Hebrew]

———. *Commentary on the Torah*. [Reprinted in various standard editions of the Hebrew Bible.] [Hebrew]

Ibn Ezra, Moses. "Le kitab Al Mouhadara Wa-l-Moudhakara de Moise B. Ezra et ses sources," edited by M. Schreiner. *REV* XXI (1890): 98–117; XXII (1891): 239–49.

———. *Shirat Yisrael*. Translated by B. Halper. Leipzig, 1924.

———. *Selected Poems*. Translated by S. Solis-Cohen. Philadelphia: The Jewish Publication Society of America, 1934.

———. *Secular Poems*. Edited by H. Brody. 2 vols. Berlin/Jerusalem: Shoken, 1935–1942. [Hebrew]

———. *Secular Poems*. Edited by Dan Pagis. Vol. 3. Shoken: Jerusalem, 1977. [Hebrew]

———. *Sefer haIyyunim v'haDiyyunim*. Edited by A. Halkin [Hebrew translation of *Kitab al-Muhadara wa'l-Mudhakara/ The Book of Conversations and Memories*; Ibn Ezra's poetics originally written in Arabic.] Jerusalem: Hotsa'at mekitse nirdamim, 1975. [Hebrew]

Ibn Gabriol, Solomon. *Selected Religious Poems*. Translated by Israel Zangwill. Philadelphia: The Jewish Publication Society of America, 1932.

———. *The Kingly Crown*. Translated by B. Lewis. London: Valentine Mitchell, 1961.

———. *The Liturgical Poetry of Rabbi Solomon Ibn Gabriol*. Edited by D. Yarden. 2 vols. Dov Yarden: Jerusalem, 1971–1972. [Hebrew]

———. *The Secular Poetry of Rabbi Solomon Ibn Gabriol*. Edited by D. Yarden. 2 vols. Dov Yarden: Jerusalem, 1975–1976. [Hebrew]

Ibn Gikatilla, Yosef. *Sha'arei Orah*. Edited by Joseph ben Shlomo. Jerusalem: The Bialik Institute, 1975. [Hebrew]

Ibn Habib, Moshe. *Darkhei No'am*. Venice: Daniel Bomberg, 1546. [Hebrew]

Ibn Janah, Yonah. *Opuscules et traits*. Edited by J. and H. Derenbourg. Paris, 1880.

———. *Sefer ha'Shorashim*. Edited by B.Z. Bacher. Berlin: Mekize Nirdamim, 1896. [Hebrew]

Ibn Khaldun. *The Muqaddimah*. Edited by F. Rosenthal. 3 vols. New York: Pantheon, 1958.

Ibn Nagrela, Samuel (Shmuel ha'Nagid). *Jewish Prince in Moslem Spain*. Translated by L.J. Weinberger. Tuscaloosa: University of Alabama Press, 1973.

———. *Diwan*. Edited by D. Yarden. 2 vols. Jerusalem: Hebrew Union College Press, 1966–1982. [Hebrew]

Ibn Pakuda, Yahya. *Book of Direction to the "Duties of the Heart."* Translated by Menahem Mansoor. London: Routledge and Kegan 1973.

Ibn Sahula, Isaac. *Mashal haQadmoni*. Edited by Y. Zamora. Tel Aviv: Mahberot le-Sifrut, 1953. [Hebrew]

———. "The Sorcerer," trans. Raymond P. Scheindlin. *FICTION* 7, nos. 1/2 (1983); republished in *Rabbinic Fantasies: Imaginative Narratives from Classical Hebrew Literature*, edited by David Stern and Mark Jay Mirsky, 295–312. New Haven: Yale University Press, 1990.
Ibn Verga, Solomon. *Shevet Yehuda*. Edited by F. Baer with notes by E. Shohet. Jerusalem: New York: Schocken, 1947. [Hebrew]
Ibn Zabara, Meir. *The Book of Delight*. Translated by Moses Hadas. New York: Columbia University Press, 1932.
Immanuel haRomi. *Tophet and Eden*. Translated by Herman Gollancz. London: University of London Press, 1921.
———. *Machberot Immanuel haRomi*. Edited by D. Yarden. Mossad Bialik: Jerusalem, 1957. [Hebrew]
———. *Introduction to the Book of Proverbs with the Commentary of Immanuel of Rome*. Edited by David Goldstein. Jerusalem: Magnes, 1981. [Hebrew]
———. *The Machberot. Fourteenth Canto: The Inheritance*. Translated by Victor Emmanuel Reichert. Cincinnati: Hebrew Union College Press, 1982.
Jerusalem Bible. Jerusalem: Koren, 1977.
Jessurun, Rehuel. *Dialogo dos Montes*. London: Tamesis, 1975.
Jewish Publication Society of America, ed. *The Holy Scriptures According to the Masoretic Text*. 2 vols. Philadelphia: Jewish Publication Society of America, 1979.
Leon, Judah Messer. *The Book of the Honeycomb's Flow*. Edited and translated by Isaac Rabinowitz. Ithaca: Cornell University Press, 1983.
Leviant, Curt, ed. and trans. *King Artus: A Hebrew Arthurian Romance of 1279*. Assen: Van Gorcum, 1969.
Llubera, J. Gonzales, ed. *Santob de Carrión: Proverbios Morales*. Cambridge: Hispanic Seminary of Medieval Studies, 1947.
Maimonides, Moses. *The Guide for the Perplexed*. Translated by Shlomo Pines. Chicago: University of Chicago Press, 1963.
———. *Ethical Writings*. Edited by Raymond L. Weiss and Charles Butterworth. New York: Dover, 1983.

Matt, Daniel Chanan, ed. *Zohar: The Book of Enlightenment.* New York: Paulist Press, 1983.
Najara, Yisrael. *Zemirot Yisrael.* Tel Aviv: Mahberot Le-Sifrut, 1945. [Hebrew]
Nawood, N.J., trans. *The Koran.* Harmondsworth: Penguin, 1974.
Nieto, David. *Mateh Dan y Segunda Parte del Cuzari.* London, 1714.
———. *De la Divina Providencia.* London, 1716.
———. *The Rod of Judgement.* Translated by L. Loewe. London, 1842.
Oliveyra, Shlomo. *Ayelet Ahavim.* Amsterdam, 1657. [Hebrew]
Onkineirah, David. *Poems.* Edited by Y. Patai. Jerusalem: Land of Yisrael Publishers, 1937–38. [Hebrew]
Petrarca, Francesco. *Canzoniere.* Edited by Gianfranco Contini. Torino: Einaudi, 1964.
Ruiz, Juan Arcipreste de Hita. *Libro de buen amor.* Madrid: Espasa Calpe, 1963.
Rumi, Jalaladdin. *Selected Poems from the Divani Shamsi Tabriz.* Edited and translated by R.A. Nicholson. Cambridge, 1898.
Samaw'al Ibn 'Adiya. *Der Diwan des as Samawal Ibn Adija.* Edited by J.W Hirschberg. Kraków: Polskiej Akademii Umiejętności, 1931. [Arabic]
Shawat, Fradji. *The Poems of Rabbi Fradji Shawat.* Edited by Ephraim Hazan. Jerusalem: The Ben Zvi Institute, 1976. [Hebrew]
Sheperd, Sanford, trans. *Shem Tov: His World and His Words.* Miami: Ediciones Universal, 1978.
Sulam, Sarah Copia. *Sonetti Editi et Inediti.* Bologna, 1887.
Tishby, Yeshaiah, ed. *Pirkei Zohar.* 2 vols. Jerusalem: The Bialik Institute, 1970. [Hebrew]
Usque, Salomon. *De los sonetos, canciones, mandriales y sextinas del gran Poeta y Orador Francisco Petrarca. Traduzidos de Toscano por Salomon Usque, Hebreo.* Venice: Nicolao Bevilaqua, 1567.

———. *Consolation for the Tribulations of Israel*. Translated by Martin Cohen. Philadelphia: The Jewish Publication Society of America, 1977.
Zacuto, Moshe. *Yesod 'Olam*. Edited by A. Berliner. Kraków, 1874. [Hebrew]
Zarco, Yehuda. *Lechem Yehuda*. Constantinople, 1560. [Hebrew]

III. Modern Sources: Single Authors

Abdullah, Yahya Taher. *The Mountain of Green Tea*. Translated by Denys Johnson-Davies. London: Heinemann, 1984.
Abouzeid, Leila. *The Year of the Elephant*. Translated by Barbara Parmenter. Austin: Center for Middle Eastern Studies, 1989.
Accad, Evelyne. *Léxcisée*. Translated by David Bruner. Washington, DC: Three Continents, 1989.
Adonis. *The Blood of Adonis*. Translated by Samuel Hazo. Pittsburgh: University of Pittsburgh Press, 1971.
Adnan, Etel. "In the Heart of the Heart of Another Country." *Mundus Artium* 10, no. 1 (1977): 20–34.
———. *Sitt Marie Rose*. Sausalito: Post-Apollo, 1982.
———. *The Indian Never Had a Horse and Other Poems*. Sausalito: Post-Apollo, 1985.
———. *Journey to Mount Tamalpais*. Sausalito: Post-Apollo, 1986.
———. *The Arab Apocalypse*. Sausalito: Post-Apollo, 1989.
———. *The Spring Flowers Own and Manifestations of the Voyage*. Sausalito: Post-Apollo, 1990.
Aguilar, Grace. *Women of Israel*. 2 vols. New York: Appleton, 1854.
Albeg, Yehezkel Hai. *Diwan: Anthology of Verses, Poems, and Lyrics*. Encino: Y.H. El-Beg, 1983. [Hebrew]
Almanzi, Yosef. *Higayon beKinor*. Padova, 1839. [Hebrew]
———. *Nezem Zahav*. Padova, 1858. [Hebrew]
Angel, Moses. *The Law of Sinai and Its Appointed Times*. London: William Tegg, 1858.

Artom, Benjamin. *Sermons.* London: Trubner, 1873.
Ballas, Shimon. *The Transit Camp.* Tel Aviv: Am Oved, 1964. [Hebrew]
———. *Facing the Wall.* Masada: Ramat Gan 1969. [Hebrew]
———. *Downtown.* Tel Aviv: Sifriyat Tarmil, 1979. [Hebrew]
———. *A Locked Room.* Tel Aviv: Zmora Biton, 1980. [Hebrew]
———. "Imaginary Childhood." *The Jerusalem Quarterly* 21 (Fall 1981): 55.
———. *Last Winter.* Jerusalem: Keter, 1984. [Hebrew]
———. *The Heir.* Tel Aviv: Zmora Biton, 1987. [Hebrew]
———. *The Other One.* Tel Aviv: Zmora Biton, 1991. [Hebrew]
Benamozegh, Elia. *Em l'Miqra.* 5 vols. Livorno: Bi-defus E. ben Amozeg va-haverav, 1862–1865. [Hebrew]
———. *Cinque Conferenze sulla Pentecoste.* Livorno, 1886.
———. *Scritti scelti.* Edited by Alfredo S. Toaff. Rome: La Rassegna mensile d'Israel, 1954.
Barakat, Halim. *Six Days.* Translated by Bassam Frangieh and Scott McGehee. Washington, DC: Three Continents, 1990.
Ben Jalloun, Tahar. *Moha le fou. Moha le sage.* Paris: Éditions de Seuil, 1978.
———. *L'enfant de sable.* Paris: Éditions du Seuil, 1985.
Bitton, Erez. *Mincha Marokayit.* Tel Aviv: 'Eqed, 1976. [Hebrew]
———. *The Book of Mint Tea.* Tel Aviv: 'Eqed, 1979. [Hebrew]
———. *A Bird Between Continents.* Tel Aviv: HaKibbutz HaMeyuchad, 1990. [Hebrew]
Burla, Yehuda. *Collected Works.* 8 vols. Davar-Massada: Tel Aviv, 1962. [Hebrew]
———. *In Darkness Striving.* Translated by Joseph Schachter. Jerusalem: Israel Universities Press, 1968.
Canetti, Elias. *Crowds and Power.* Translated by Carol Stewart. New York: Seabury, 1978.
———. *The Human Province.* Translated by Joachim Neugroschel. New York: Farrar, Straus, and Giroux, 1978.
———. *The Tongue Set Free.* Translated by Joachim Neugroschel. New York: Seabury, 1979.

Canetti, Veza. *Yellow Street.* Translated by Ian Mitchell. New York: New Directions, 1990.

Castelete, Rachel. *Esta Gimka es el Tesoro de Rachael Casteleta Ija de Jacov Yona.* London, 1959.

Charef, Mehdi. *Tea in the Harem.* Translated by Ed Emery. London: Serpent's Tail, 1989.

Chetrit, Nehorai Meir. *La terreur du rêve.* Tel Aviv: Papyrus, 1983.

———. *Le diable du desert.* Tel Aviv: Papyrus, 1987.

Chetrit, Sami Shalom. *Opening.* Tel Aviv: 'Eqed, 1988. [Hebrew]

———. *Poems in an Other Land.* Unpublished manuscript, 1992. [Hebrew]

Chraïbi, Driss. *La mère du printemps.* Paris: Éditions du Seuil, 1982.

———. *The Simple Past.* Translated by Hugh A. Carter. Washington, DC: Three Continents, 1990.

Cixous, Hélène. *Dedans.* Paris: Des Femmes, 1986.

Cohen, Albert. *Solal.* Paris: Gallimard, 1930.

———. *Solal.* Translated by Wilfred Benson. New York: Dutton, 1933.

———. *Mangeclous.* Paris: Gallimard, 1938.

———. *La livre de ma mère.* Paris: Gallimard, 1954.

Cossery, Albert. *Proud Beggars.* Translated by Thomas W. Cushing. Los Angeles: Black Sparrow, 1981.

Darwish, Mahmoud. *The Music of Human Flesh.* Translated by Denys Johnson-Davies. London: Heinemann, 1980.

———. *Memorial to Forgetfulness.* [Translator not specified]. Jerusalem: Schocken, 1989. [Hebrew]

Davičo, Haim C. *Sa Jalije.* Belgrade, 1898. [Serbian]

Djebar, Assia. *L'amour, La fantasia.* Paris: J.C. Lattes, 1985.

———. *Fantasia: An Algerian Cavalcade.* Translated by Dorothy S. Blair. London: Quartet, 1985.

———. *Femmes d'Alger dans leur appartement.* Paris: Des Femmes, 1986.

Elia, Lucien. *Les ratés de la diaspora.* Paris: Flammarion, 1969.

Eliachar, Eliahu. *Living with Palestinians.* Jerusalem: Council of the Sephardic Community of Jerusalem, 1975. [Hebrew]

———. *Existing with Jews.* Jerusalem: Marcus, 1980. [Hebrew]
Elkayam, Shelly. *Song of the Architect.* Tel Aviv: Zemora Bitan, 1987.
Forrokhzaad, Foroogh. *A Rebirth.* Translated by David Martin. Lexington: Mazda, 1985.
Genet, Jean. *Prisoner of Love.* Translated by Barbara Bray. London: Picador, 1990.
Ghali, Waguih. *Beer in the Snooker Club.* New York: New Amsterdam Books/The Meredith Press, 1987.
Ghitani, Gamal al-. *Zayni Barakat.* Translated by Farouk Abdel Wahab. New York: Penguin, 1988.
Goren, Itshak Gormezano. *An Alexandrian Summer.* Tel Aviv: 'Am 'Oved, 1978. [Hebrew]
———. *Blanche.* Tel Aviv: Am Oved, 1986. [Hebrew]
Goytisolo, Juan. *Count Julian.* Translated by Helen R. Lane. New York: Viking, 1977.
———. *Juan the Landless.* Translated by Helen R. Lane. New York: Viking, 1977.
———. *Forbidden Territory: The Memoirs of Juan Goytisolo 1931–1956.* Translated by Peter Bush. San Francisco: North Point, 1989.
———. *Realms of Strife: The Memoirs of Juan Goytisolo, 1957–1982.* Translated by Peter Bush. San Francisco: North Point, 1990.
Habiby, Emile. *The Secret Life of Saeed the Pessoptimist.* Translated by Salma Khadra Jayyusi and Trevor Le Gassick. London: Zed Press, 1985.
———. *Akhtiyeh.* Tel Aviv: 'Am 'Oved, 1988. [Hebrew]
Hareven, Shulamith. *City of Many Days.* Translated by Hillel Halkin (with the author). New York: Doubleday, 1977.
Hassoun, Jacques. *Fragments de la langue maternelle.* Paris: Payot, 1979.
———. *Alexandries.* Paris: Éditions Decouverte, 1983.

———. *Les surnoms de l'Absente.* Paris: Lieu Commun, 1983.

Hawi, Khalil. *Naked in Exile: The Threshing Floors of Hunger.* Translated by Adnan Haydar and Michael Beard. Washington, DC: Three Continents, 1984.

Hedayat, Sadeq. *The Blind Owl.* Translated by D.P. Costello. London: John Calder, 1957.

Hess, Amira. *And the Moon Drips Madness.* Tel Aviv: Am Oved, 1984. [Hebrew]

Hetata, Sherif. *The Net.* Translated by Sherif Hetata. London: Zed Books, 1986.

Hikmet, Nazim. *Human Landscapes.* Translated by Randy Blasing and Mutlu Konuk. New York: Persea, 1982.

Hussein, Taha. *An Egyptian Childhood.* Translated by E.H. Paxton. London: Heinemann, 1981.

Idris, Yusuf. *The Cheapest Nights.* Translated by Wadida Wassef. Washington, DC: Three Continents, 1989.

Jabbour, Hala Deeb. *A Woman of Nazareth.* Oakton: Virgina, 1986.

Jabès, Edmond. *Je bâtis ma demeure.* Paris: Gallimard, 1959.

———. *The Book of Questions I-VII.* Translated by Rosemarie Waldrop. Middletown: Wesleyan University, 1972–1985.

———. "Interview with Paul Auster." *Montemora* 6 (1979): 41–55.

———. *Du désert au livre* (with Marcel Cohen). Paris: Belfond, 1980.

———. "An Interview with Edmond Jabès Conducted by Jason Wiess." *Conjunctions* 9 (1986): 128–161.

———. *The Book of Dialogue.* Translated by Rosemarie Waldrop. Middletown: Wesleyan University Press, 1987.

———. *If There Were Anywhere But Desert: Selected Poems.* Translated by Keith Waldrop. Barrytown: Station Hill, 1988.

———. *From the Desert to the Book: Dialogues with Marcel Cohen.* Translated by Pierre Joris. Barrytown: Station Hill, 1990.

———. *The Book of Resemblances.* Translated by Rosemarie Waldrop. Hanover and London: Wesleyan University Press/ University Press of New England, 1990.

———. *The Book of Resemblances 2: Intimations/The Desert.* Translated by Rosemarie Waldrop. Hanover and London: Wesleyan University Press/University Press of New England, 1991.

Jabra, Jabra Ibrahim. *The Ship.* Translated by Adnan Haydar and Roger Allen. Washington, DC: Three Continents, 1985.

Kahana-Carmon, Amalia. *And Moon in the Valley of Ayalon.* Tel Aviv: HaKibbutz HaMeyuhad, 1971. [Hebrew]

———. *Magnetic Fields.* Tel Aviv: HaKibbutz HaMeyuhad, 1971. [Hebrew]

———. *Under One Roof.* Tel Aviv: Sifriyat Po'alim, 1971. [Hebrew]

Kahanoff, Jacqueline Shohet. *Jacob's Ladder.* London: Harvill, 1951.

———. *From the East the Sun.* Tel Aviv: Yariv/Haydar, 1978. [Hebrew]

———. "Childhood in Egypt." *The Jerusalem Quarterly* 36 (1985): 31–41.

Kanafani, Ghassan. *Men in the Sun.* Translated by Hilary Kirkpatrick. London: Heinemann, 1972.

———. *Palestine's Children.* Translated by Barbara Harlow. London: Heinemann, 1984.

———. *All That's Left to You.* Translated by May Jayyusi and Jeremy Reed. Austin: Center for Middle Eastern Studies, 1990.

Kateb, Yacine. *Nedjma.* Translated by Bernard Aresu. Charlottesville: University Press of Virginia, 1991.

Kattan, Naim. *Farewell, Babylon.* Translated by Sheila Fishman. New York: Taplinger, 1980.

Kayat, Claude. *Mohammed Cohen: The Adventures of an Arabian Jew.* New York: Bergh Publishing, 1989.

Khalife, Saher. *Wild Thorns.* Translated by Trevor Le Gassick and Elizabeth Fernea. London: Al Saqi, 1986.

Kharrat, Edwar al-. *City of Saffron.* Translated by Frances Liardet. London: Quartet, 1989.

Khatibi, Abdelkabir. *Love in Two Languages.* Translated by Richard Howard. Minneapolis: University of Minnesota Press, 1990.

Khatibi, Abdelkabir, and Jacques Hassoun. *Le même livre.* Paris: Éditions de l'Éclat, 1985.

Khoury, Elias. *Little Mountain.* Translated by Maia Tabet. Minneapolis: University of Minnesota Press, 1989.

Levy, Raphael (Ryvel). *L'enfant de l'Oukla et autre contes de ghetto.* Paris: J.C. Lattes, 1980.

Maalouf, Amin. *Leo Africanus.* Translated by Peter Sluglett. New York: New Amsterdam, 1992.

Mahfouz, Nagib. *Midaq Alley.* Translated by Trevor LeGassick. London: Heinemann, 1975.

———. *Miramar.* Translated by Fatma Moussa-Mahmoud. Cairo: American University of Cairo Press, 1978.

———. *Children of Gebelawi.* Translated by Phillip Stewart. London: Heinemann, 1981.

———. *The Beginning and the End.* Translated by Ramses Awad. New York: Anchor, 1989.

———. *Palace Walk.* Translated by William Maynard Hutchins and Olive E. Kenny. New York: Anchor, 1991.

———. *Palace of Desire.* Translated by William Maynard Hutchins, Lorne M. Kenny, and Olive E. Kenny. New York: Anchor, 1992.

———. *Sugar Street.* Translated by William Maynard Hutchins and Angele Botros Samaan. New York: Doubleday, 1992.

Makdisi, Jean Said. *Beirut Fragments: A War Memoir.* New York: Persea, 1990.

Matvejević, Predrag. *Mediteranski Brevijar.* Zagreb: Grafički Zavod Hrvatske, 1990. [Croatian]

Meddeb, Abdelwahab. *Phantasia.* Paris: Sindbad, 1987.

———. *Talismano.* Paris: Sindbad, 1987.

———. *Tombeau d'Ibn Arabi.* Paris: Sillages, 1987.

Medina, Shalom. *The Messiah from Yemen.* Tel Aviv: Aviner, 1989. [Hebrew]

Mellah, Fawzi. *Elissa.* Translated by Howard Curtis. London: Quartet, 1990.

Memmi, Albert. *The Pillar of Salt.* Translated by Edouard Roditi. New York: Criterion, 1955.
———. *The Scorpion.* Translated by Eleanor Levieux. Chicago: O'Hara, 1971.
Mikhael, Sami. *Refuge.* Tel Aviv: Am Oved, 1979. [Hebrew]
———. *A Trumpet in the Wadi.* Tel Aviv: 'Am 'Oved, 1987. [Hebrew]
———. *Refuge.* Translated by Edward Grossman. Philadelphia: The Jewish Publication Society of America, 1988.
Modarressi, Taghi. *The Pilgrim's Rules of Etiquette.* New York: Doubleday, 1989.
Morpurgo, Rachel. *'Ugav Rachel.* Kraków, 1890. [Hebrew]
Munif, Abdelrahman. *Cities of Salt.* Translated by Peter Theroux. New York: Vintage, 1989.
Nahum, Andre. *Partir en Kappara.* Paris: Piranhas Editions, 1977.
Nakash, Samir. *The Day the World Was Conceived and Aborted.* Translated by Ruth Naqqash. Tel Aviv: Sifriat Poalim, 1985. [Hebrew]
Nicoïdski, Clarisse. *Los ojus, las manus, la boca.* Loubressar Bretenoux: Braad Editions, 1978.
———. *Couvre-feux.* Paris: Editions Ramsay, 1981.
Pavić, Milorad. *Dictionary of the Khazars.* Translated by Christina Pribićević-Zorić. New York: Knopf, 1988.
———. *Hazarski Rećnik.* Belgrade: Prosveta, 1990. [Serbian]
Rejwan, Nissim. "Life among Muslims: A Memoir." *Present Tense* (Autumn 1981): 43–46.
Rifaat, Alifa. *Distant View of a Minaret and Other Stories.* Translated by Denys Johnson-Davies. London: Quartet, 1985.
Roditi, Edouard. *Delights of Turkey.* New York: New Directions, 1977.
———. *Thrice Chosen.* Los Angeles: Black Sparrow, 1981.
Saadawi, Nawal al-. *Woman at Point Zero.* Translated by Sherif Hetata. London: Zed, 1983.
———. *God Dies by the Nile.* Translated by Sherif Hetata. London: Zed, 1985.

———. *Memoirs of a Woman Doctor: A Novel*. Translated by Catherine Cobham. San Francisco: City Lights, 1989.
Saba, Umberto. *Poesie e prose scelte*. Milan: Mondadori, 1966.
Saffar as-, Muhammad. *Disorienting Encounters: Travels of a Moroccan Scholar in France 1845–1846 — The Voyage of Muhammad as-Saffar*. Edited and translated by Susan Gilson Miller. Berkeley: University of California Press, 1992.
Saleh, Tayib. *Season of Migration to the North*. Translated by Denys Johnson-Davies. London: Heinemann, 1976.
Samokovlija, Isaac. *Pripovijetke*. Sarajevo: Svjetlost, 1951. [Serbo-Croatian]
Selimović, Mesa. *Derviš i smrt*. Zagreb: Školska Knjiga, 1974. [Serbo-Croatian]
Serri, Brakha. *Seventy Wandering Poems*. Jerusalem: Mahberet, 1983. [Hebrew]
Shaarawi, Huda. *Harem Years*. Translated by Margot Badran. London: Virago, 1986.
Shehade, Raja. *The Third Way*. London: Quartet, 1982.
Shami, Itshaq. *Collected Stories*. Tel Aviv: Neuman, 1971. [Hebrew]
Shammas, Anton. *Arabesques*. Translated by Vivian Eden. New York: Harper and Row, 1988.
Shamosh, Amnon. *My Sister Is the Bride*. Tel Aviv: Massada, 1978. [Hebrew]
Sheikh, Hanan al-. *The Story of Zahra*. Translated by Peter Ford. London: Pan, 1987
———. *Women of Sand and Myrrh*. Translated by Catherine Cobham. New York: Anchor, 1989.
Someck, Ronny. *7 Lines on the Wonder of the Yarkon*. Tel Aviv: Opatowski, 1987. [Hebrew]
———. *Panther*. Tel Aviv: Zmora Biton, 1989. [Hebrew]
Swissa, Albert. *The Bound*. Tel Aviv: HaKibbutz HaMeyuhad, 1990. [Hebrew]
Tawil, Raymonda. *My Home, My Prison*. London: Zed, 1983.
Traboulsi, Fawwaz. "Beirut-Guernica: A City and A Painting." *Middle East Report* 154 (September-October 1988): 29–37.
Trigano, Shmuel. *Le récit de la disparue*. Paris: Gallimard, 1977.

Tuqan, Fadwa. *A Mountainous Journey: A Poet's Autobiography*. Translated by Olive Kenny. St Paul: Greywolf, 1990.

Turki, Fawaz. *The Disinherited: Journal of a Palestine Exile*. New York: Monthly Review, 1974.

Ungaretti, Giuseppe. *Vita d'un uomo*. Milan: Mondadori, 1966.

Yehoshua, A.B. *Five Seasons*. Translated by Hillel Halkin. New York: Dutton, 1990.

———. *Mr. Mani*. Tel Aviv: HaKibbutz HaMeyuhad, 1990. [Hebrew]

———. *The Continuing Silence of a Poet*. New York: Penguin, 1991.

———. *Mr. Mani*. Translated by Hillel Halkin. New York: Doubleday, 1992.

Yehoshua, Ya'akob. *Childhood in Old Jerusalem*. 6 vols. Jerusalem: Rubin Mass, 1966–1979. [Hebrew]

Yona, Yacob. *The Judeo-Spanish Ballad Chapbooks of Yakob Abraham Yona*. Edited by Samuel Gordon Armistead and Joe Silverman. Berkeley: University of California Press, 1971.

IV. Literary Backgrounds/Poetics

Abu Deeb, Kamal. *Al-Jurjani's Theory of Poetic Imagery*. London: Aris & Phillips, Ltd., 1979.

Accad, Evelyne. *Sexuality and War: Literary Masks of the Middle East*. New York: New York University Press, 1990.

Adonis. *Mujaddira lish-shi'r al-'arabi*. Beirut, 1971. [Arabic]

———. *Introduction à la poétique arabe*. Translated by Bassam Tahan and Anna Wade Minkowski. Paris: Sindbad, 1985.

———. *An Introduction to Arab Poetics*. Translated by Catherine Cobham. London: Saqi Books, 1990.

Alcalay, Ammiel. "The Quill's Embroidery." *Parnassus* (Spring/Summer 1983): 85–115.

———. "Who's Afraid of Mahmoud Darwish?" *Middle East Report* 154 (September/October 1988): 27–28.

———. "Israel and the Levant: 'Wounded Kinship's Last Resort.'" *Middle East Report* 159 (July-August 1989): 18–23.

———. "Gulf States of Mind: Learning to Read Arab Fiction." *Village Voice Literary Supplement* (June 1991): 15.

———. "Too Much Past, No Future: Sugar Street by Naguib Mahfouz." *New York Times Book Review*, March 22, 1992, 17.

Appignanesi, Lisa and Sara Maitland, eds. *The Rushdie File.* Syracuse: Syracuse University Press, 1990.

Arkin, Alexander Habib. *La Influencia de la Exégesis Hebrea en los commentarios Biblicos de Fray Luis de Leon.* Madrid: Instituto Benito Arias Montano, 1966.

Ashcroft, Bill, Gareth Griffiths, and Hellen Tiffin. *The Empire Writes Back: Theory and Practice in Post-Colonial Literatures.* London and New York: Routledge, 1989.

Ashrawi, Hanan Mikhail. *Contemporary Palestinian Literature Under Occupation.* Bir Zeit: Bir Zeit University Press, 1976.

Ballas, Shimon. *Arab Literature under the Shadow of War.* Tel Aviv: Am Oved, 1978. [Hebrew]

Barukh, Kalmi. *Izabrana djela.* Sarajevo: Svjetlost, 1972. [Serbo-Croatian]

Bencheikh, Jamal Eddine. *Poétique arabe.* Paris: Éditions Anthropos, 1975.

———. "Ecriture et ideologie (la littérature algérienne horizon 2000)." *Les Temps Modernes* (October 1977): 355–77.

Blachere, R. *Histoire de la littérature arabe.* 3 vols. Paris, 1952–1956.

Blau, J. *The Emergence and Linguistic Background of Judeo-Arabic: A Study of the Origins of Middle Arabic.* Oxford: Oxford University Press, 1963.

Brann, Ross. *The Compunctuous Poet: Cultural Ambiguity and Hebrew Poetry in Muslim Spain.* Baltimore: Johns Hopkins University Press, 1991.

Butor, Michel. *The Spirit of Mediterranean Places.* Translated by Lydia Davis. Marlboro: Marlboro, 1986.

Cansinos-Asséns, Raphael. *Los judíos en la literatura española.* Buenos Aires: Columna, 1937.

———. *Los judíos en Sefarad: Episodios y simbolos.* Buenos Aires: Editorial Israel, 1950.

———. "Cervantes y los Israelitas Españoles." In *España y los judíos españoles: El retorno del éxodo*, 125–44. Tortosa: Casa Editorial Monclús, 1919.

———. "Estudio Literario-Critico de Las Mil y Una Noches," in *Libro de las Mil y Una Noches*, Vol. 1, 11–376. Madrid: Aguilar, 1969.

Cohen, Adir. *An Ugly Face in the Mirror.* Tel Aviv: Reshafim, 1985. [Hebrew]

Cohen, Dalia. *East and West in Music.* Jerusalem: Magnes, 1986.

Cooke, Miriam. *War's Other Voices: Women Writers on the Lebanese Civil War.* Cambridge: Cambridge University Press, 1988.

Dana, Yosef. *Poetics of Medival Hebrew Literature According to Moses Ibn Ezra.* Jerusalem: Dvir, 1982. [Hebrew]

Darwish, Mahmoud, with Simone Bitton et al. *Palestine, mon pays: l'affaire du poème.* Paris: Éditions de Minuit, 1988.

Diamond, James. *Homeland or Holy Land? The "Canaanite Critique" of Israel.* Bloomington: University of Indiana Press, 1986.

Domb, Risa. *The Arab in Hebrew Prose, 1911–1942.* London: Valentine Mitchell, 1982.

Dronke, Peter. *The Medieval Lyric.* New York: Harper and Row, 1964.

———. *Medieval Latin and the Rise of the European Love-Lyric.* 2 vols. Oxford: Oxford University Press, 1965–1966.

Einbinder, Susan. "The Current Debate on the Muwashshah." *Prooftexts* 9 (1989): 161–77.

El-Asmar, Fouzi. *Through the Looking Glass: Arab Stereotypes in Children's Literature.* London: Zed, 1986.

Farmer, Henry George. *A History of Arabian Music to the XIIth Century.* London: Luzae, 1929.

———. *Historical Facts for the Arabian Musical Influence.* London: William Reeves, 1930.

———. *Saadyia Gaon and Music.* London, 1943.

———. "The Music of Islam." In *The New Oxford History of Music, Vol 1: Ancient and Oriental Music*, edited by Egon Wellesz, 421–77. London: Oxford University Press, 1957.

———. *The Oriental Musical Influence and Jewish Geniza Fragments on Music*. New York: Hinrichsen Edition, 1964.

———. *The Sources of Arabian Music*. Leiden: Brill, 1965.

Faur, José. "Some General Observations on the Character of Classical Jewish Literature." *Journal of Jewish Studies* 37 (1977): 30–45.

———. *Golden Dots with Silver Doves*. Bloomington: Indiana University Press, 1986.

Feldman, Yael S. "Feminism Under Siege: The Vicarious Selves of Israeli Women Writers." *Prooftexts* 10 (1990): 493–574.

Fleischer, Ezra. *Hebrew Liturgical Poetry in the Middle Ages*. Jerusalem: Keter, 1975. [Hebrew]

———. "On Dunash ben Labrat, His Wife and Son: New Light on the Beginnings of the Spanish School." *Jerusalem Studies in Hebrew Literature* 5 (1984): 189–202. [Hebrew]

Franco, Moise. *Histoire et littérature juive pays par pays*. 2 vols. Paris: Nathan, 1905.

Gertner, Meir. "On Translating Medieval Hebrew Writing." *Journal of the Royal Asiatic Society* 3/4 (1962–63): 163–93.

Gilman, Stephen. *The Spain of Fernando de Rojas*. Princeton: Princeton University Press, 1972.

Gontard, Marc. *Violence du texte: littérature marocaine de langue française*. Paris: l'Harmattan, 1981.

Gover, Yerah. *Zionism: The Limits of Moral Discourse*. PhD Dissertation, CUNY Graduate Center, 1992.

Goytisolo, Juan. *Disidencias*. Barcelona: Editorial Seix Barral, 1978.

Grunebaum, G.E. von. *A Tenth-Century Document of Arab Literary Theory and Criticism*. Chicago: University of Chicago Press, 1950.

Hakak, Lev. *Inferiors and Superiors: Oriental Jews in the Hebrew Short Story*. Jerusalem: Kiryat Sefer, 1981. [Hebrew]

Hamori, Andras. *On the Art of Medieval Arabic Literature*. Princeton: Princeton University Press, 1974.

Harlow, Barbara. *Resistance Literature.* New York: Methuen, 1987.

Hazzan, Ephraim. *The Poetics of the Sephardi Piyyut According to the Poetics of Yehuda haLevi.* Jerusalem: Magnes, 1986. [Hebrew]

Hever, Hanan. "Minority Discourse of a National Minority: Israeli Fiction of the Early Sixties." *Prooftexts* 10 (1990): 129–47.

Hirschfeld, Hartwig. *Literary History of Hebrew Grammarians and Lexicographers.* London: Oxford University Press, 1926.

Jayyusi, Salma Khadra. *Trends and Movements in Modern Arab Poetry.* 2 vols. Leiden: Brill, 1977.

Kahana-Carmon, Amalia. "1948 and After." *Modern Hebrew Literature* 10, nos. 1/2 (Fall/Winter 1984): 8.

Karpeles, Gustav. *Jewish Literature and Other Essays.* Philadelphia: The Jewish Publication Society of America, 1985.

Kugel, James L. *The Idea of Biblical Poetry: Parallelism and its History.* New Haven: Yale University Press, 1981.

Landau, Jacob M. "Bittersweet Nostalgia: Memoirs of Jewish Immigrants from the Arab Countries." *Middle East Journal* 35, no. 2 (1981): 229–35.

Levin, Gabriel. "What Different Things Link Up: Hellenism in Contemporary Hebrew Poetry." *Prooftexts* 5 (1985): 221–43.

Lida de Malkiel, Maria Rosa. *Two Spanish Masterpieces: The "Book of Good Love" and "The Celestina."* Urbana-Champaign: University of Illinois Press, 1961.

Lyall, Charles. "The Pictorial Aspects of Ancient Arabian Poetry." *Journal of the Royal Asiatic Society* XLIV (1912): 133–52.

———. "The Relation of the Old Arabian Poetry to the Hebrew Literature of the Old Testament." *Journal of the Royal Asiatic Society* XLVI (1914): 253–66.

Malti-Douglas, Fedwa. *Woman's Body, Woman's Word: Gender and Discourse in Arabo-Islamic Writing.* Princeton: Princeton University Press, 1991.

Mamorstein, Emile. "An Iraqi Jewish Writer in the Holy Land," *The Jewish Journal of Sociology* 6, no. 1 (1964): 91–102.

Matalon, Abraham. *The Hebrew Pronounciation in Its Struggle.* Tel Aviv: Hadar, 1979. [Hebrew]

Menocal, María Rosa. *The Arabic Role in Medieval Literary History: A Forgotten Heritage.* Philadelphia: University of Pennsylvania Press, 1990.

Michael, Sami. "On Being an Iraqi-Jewish Writer in Israel." *Prooftexts* 4 (1984): 23–33.

———. "Zionist Arabesques." *The Jerusalem Quarterly* 45 (Winter 1988): 127–44.

Molho, Michael. *Literatura sefardita de Oriente.* Madrid: Instituto Arias Montano, 1960.

Morais, Sabato. *Italian Hebrew Literature.* New York: The Jewish Theological Seminary, 1926.

Moreh, Shmuel. "Live Theater in Medieval Islam." In *Studies in Islamic History and Civilization in Honour of Prof. David Ayalon,* edited by Moshe Sharon, 565–611. Leiden: Brill, 1986.

Nicholson, A.R. *A Literary History of the Arabs.* Cambridge: Cambridge University Press, 1979.

Nykl, A.R. *Hispano-Arabic Poetry.* Baltimore: J.H. Furst Co., 1946.

Nyssen, Hubert. *Lecture d'Albert Cohen.* Avignon: Alain Bartholemy and Actes Sud, 1981.

Pagis, Dan. *Secular Poetry and Poetic Theory: Moses Ibn Ezra and His Contemporaries.* Jerusalem: The Bialik Institute, 1970. [Hebrew]

———. *Change and Tradition in Secular Poetry: Spain and Italy.* Jerusalem: Keter, 1976. [Hebrew]

———. "Variety in Medieval Rhymed Narratives." In *Scripta Hiersolymitana,* Vol. XXVII, 79–98. Jerusalem: Magnes, 1978.

———. *A Secret Sealed: Hebrew Baroque Emblem Riddles from Italy and Holland.* Jerusalem: Magnes, 1986. [Hebrew]

Romero, Elena. *El teatro de los sefardies orientales.* 3 vols. Madrid: Instituto Arias Montano, 1979.

Semaan, Khalil. *Linguistics in the Middle Ages: Phonetic Studies in Early Islam.* Leiden: Brill, 1968.

Semah, David. *Four Egyptian Literary Critics*. Leiden: Brill, 1974.

Shasha, David. *Theories of Writing in Shem Tob Ardutiel's The Battle of the Pen and the Scissors*. MA Thesis, Cornell University, January 1990.

Sheperd, Sanford. "Crypto Jews in Spanish Literature." *Judaism* 19 (1970): 99–112.

———. "Prostitutes and Picaros in Inquisitional Spain." *Neohelicon* 3 (1975): 365–72.

———. *Lost Lexicon: Secret Meanings in the Vocabulary of Spanish Literature during the Inquisition*. Miami: Ediciones Universal, 1982.

———. "Notes on Sempronio's Abuse of Calixto in La Celestina." *Neohelicon* 9, no. 2 (1982): 335–41.

Slyomovics, Susan. "'To Put One's Finger in the Bleeding Wound': Palestinian Theater Under Israeli Censorship." *The Drama Review* 35, no. 2 (Summer 1991): 18–38.

Snir, Reuben. "'We Were Like Those Who Dream': Iraqi-Jewish Writers in Israel in the 1950s." *Prooftexts* 11 (1991): 153–73.

Somekh, Sasson. *The Changing Rhythm: A Study of Najib Mahfuz's Novels*. Leiden: Brill, 1973.

———. *A Literature in Search of a Language*. Tel Aviv: Tel Aviv University, 1983.

Steinschneider, M. *Jewish Literature from the 8th to the 18th Century*. London, 1857.

van Gelder, G.J.H. *Beyond the Line: Classical Arabic Literary Critics on the Coherence and Unity of the Poem*. Leiden: Brill, 1982.

Walzer, Richard. *Greek into Arabic: Essays on Islamic Philosophy*. Oxford: Oxford University Press, 1962.

Werner, Eric. *The Sacred Bridge: The Interdependence of Liturgy and Music in Synagogue and Church in the First Millennium*. New York: Columbia University Press, 1959.

Werner, Eric, with I. Sonne. "The Philosophy and Theory of Music in Judeo-Arabic Literature." *Hebrew Union College Annual* 16 (1941): 251–319, and 17 (1942/43): 511–72.

Yahuda, A.S. *The Language of the Pentateuch in Relation to Egyptian*. Oxford: Clarendon, 1933.
———. *'Eber ve'Arab*. New York: 'Ogen, 1946. [Hebrew]
Yellin, David. *Introduction to the Hebrew Poetry of the Spanish Period*. Jerusalem: Magnes, 1978. [Hebrew]
Yosef, Shaul Abdullah. *Gibeath Shaul, Being a Commentary in Hebrew on Poems of R. Juda Ha-Levi by Saul Joseph of Hongkong*. Vienna: Krauss, 1923. [Hebrew]
———. *Mishbeseth haTarshish, Being a Commentary in Hebrew of the Poetical Works of Moses Aben Ezra by Saul Joseph of Hongkong*. London: Goldston, 1926. [Hebrew]
Zafrani, Haim. *Poésie juive en Occident musulman*. Paris: Geuthner, 1977.
Zeidan, Joseph. "Myth and Symbol in the Poetry of Adunis and Yusuf Al-Khal." *Journal of Arabic Literature* (1979): 70–94.
Zumthor, Paul. *Essai de poétique médiévale*. Paris: Éditions de Seuil, 1972.
———. *Speaking of the Middle Ages*. Translated by Sarah White. Lincoln: University of Nebraska Press, 1985.

V. History, Politics, Religion, Society, Culture and Thought

Abbott, Nabia. *Two Queens of Baghdad: Mother and Wife of Harun al-Rashid*. Chicago: University of Chicago Press, 1974.
———. *Aisha: The Beloved of Mohammed*. London: Al Saqi, 1986.
Abdalla, Ahmed. *The Student Movement and National Politics in Egypt, 1923–1973*. London: Al Saqi, 1985.
Abrahams, Israel. *Jewish Life in the Middle Ages*. London: Macmillan, 1896.
Abu Hammud, Nikola Kostandi. *Directory of Geographical Names in Palestine*. Jerusalem: The Arab Studies Society, 1984. [Arabic]
Abu-Lughod, Ibrahim. *The Transformation of Palestine*. Evanston: Northwestern University Press, 1971.

———. *Arab Rediscovery of Europe: A Study in Cultural Encounters.* Princeton: Princeton University Press, 1973.
Abu-Lughod, Janet. *Cairo: 1001 Years of the City Victorious.* Princeton: Princeton University Press, 1971.
———. *Rabat: Urban Apartheid in Morocco.* Princeton: Princeton University Press, 1980.
———. *Before Euopean Hegemony: The World System A.D. 1250–1350.* New York: Oxford University Press, 1991.
Abu-Lughod, Janet, and Richard Hays, Jr., eds. *Third World Urbanization.* Chicago: Maaroufa, 1977.
Adler, Elkan Nathan. *Jews in Many Lands.* Philadelphia: The Jewish Publication Society of America, 1905.
Agnon, Shmuel Yosef. "To S.Z. Schocken after the 1929 Riots." *The Jerusalem Quarterly* 9 (Fall 1978): 46–54.
Alcalay, Ammiel. "La communauté sépharade en Israël et la processus de paix." *Perspectives Judéo-Arabes* 7 (1987): 47–85.
———. "Reorienting: Sephardim in the Middle East." *New Outlook Middle East Monthly,* January/February 1987, 51.
———. "Forbidden Territory, Promised Land." *Middle East Report* 164–165 (May-August 1990): 63–66.
———. "In True Colors." *Afterimage,* October 1991, 15.
Alloula, Malek. *The Colonial Harem.* Minneapolis: University of Minnesota Press, 1985.
And, Metin. *A History of Theater and Popular Entertainment in Turkey.* Ankara: Forum, 1963/64.
Angel, Marc. *Voices in Exile: A Study in Sephardic Intellectual History.* Hoboken: KTAV, 1991.
Ardalan, Nader, and Laleh Bakhtiar. *The Sense of Unity: The Sufi Tradition in Persian Architecture.* Chicago: University of Chicago Press, 1977.
Ashtor, Eliyahu. *The Jews of Moslem Spain.* 3 vols. Philadelphia: The Jewish Publication Society of America, 1973–1984.
———. *A Social and Economic History of the Near East in the Middle Ages.* London: University of California Press, 1976.
———. *The Jews and the Mediterranean Economy: 10th–15th Century.* London: Variorum Reprints, 1983.

Atiya, Nayra. *Khul-Khaal: Five Egyptian Women Tell Their Stories.* Cairo: American University in Cairo Press, 1984.
Baer, Itshak. *History of the Jews in Christian Spain.* 2 vols. Philadelphia: The Jewish Publication Society of America, 1966.
Bahloul, Joëlle. *Le culte de la table dressée.* Paris: Métailié, 1983.
Baron, Salo W. *A Social and Religious History of the Jews.* 12 vols. New York: Columbia University Press, 1952–1967.
Batatu, H. *The Old Social Classes and the Revolutionary Movement in Iraq: A Study of Iraq's Old Landed Commercial Classes and Its Communists, Ba'athists and Free Officers.* Princeton: Princeton University Press, 1978.
Beck, Lois, and Nikki Keddie, eds. *Women in the Muslim World.* Cambridge: Harvard University Press, 1978.
Bernardete, Maír José. *Hispanic Culture and Character of the Sephardic Jews.* New York: Hispanic Institute, 1952.
Bernal, Martin. *Black Athena: The Afroasiatic Roots of Classical Civilization, Vol. 1: The Fabrication of Ancient Greece, 1785–1985.* New Brunswick: Rutgers University Press, 1987.
Bloch, Marc. *Feudal Society.* Translated by L.A. Manyon. 2 vols. Chicago: University of Chicago Press, 1961.
Braudel, Fernand. *The Mediterranean World in the Age of Phillip II.* Translated by Siân Reynolds. 2 vols. New York: Harper and Row, 1972–1973.
Brenner, Lenni. *Zionism in the Age of the Dictators.* New York: Lawrence Hill, 1983.
Brown, Kenneth, and Jean Mohr. "Journey Through the Labyrinth: A Photographic Essay on Israel/Palestine." *Studies in Visual Communication* 8, no. 2 (Spring 1982): 2–81.
Brown, L.C., ed. *From Medina to Metropolis: Heritage and Change in the Near Eastern City.* Princeton: Darwin, 1973.
Brown, Sarah Graham. *Palestinians and Their Society, 1880–1946.* London: Quartet, 1980.
———. *Images of Women: The Portrayal of Women in the Photography of the Middle East, 1860–1950.* New York: Columbia University Press, 1988.

Chouraqui, André. *La condition juridique de l'israélite marocain.* Paris: Alliance Israelite Universelle, 1950.

———. *Between East and West: A History of the Jews in Africa.* Translated by Michael M. Bernet. Atheneum: New York, 1973.

Clot, André. *Haroun al-Rashid and the World of the Thousand and One Nights.* London: Al Saqi, 1988.

Cohen, Aharon. *Israel and the Arab World.* New York: Funk and Wagnalls, 1970.

Cohen, Jeremy. *The Friars and the Jews.* Ithaca: Cornell University Press, 1982.

Cohen, Mark R., and Abraham L. Udovitch, eds. *Jews Among Arabs: Contacts and Boundaries.* Princeton: Darwin, 1989.

Corbin, Henry. *Creative Imagination in the Sufism of Ibn Arabi.* Translated by Ralph Manheim. Princeton: Bollingen, 1981.

Corcos, David. *Studies in the History of the Jews of Morocco.* Jerusalem: Rubin Mass, 1976. [Hebrew]

Crapanzano, Vincent. *Tuhami: Portrait of a Moroccan.* Chicago: University of Chicago Press, 1980.

Creswell, K.A.C. *Early Muslim Architecture.* London: Penguin, 1958.

Cutler, Allan H. *The Jew as an Ally of the Muslim.* South Bend: Notre Dame University Press, 1986.

Daniel, Norman. *Islam, Europe, and Empire.* Edinburgh: Edinburgh University Press, 1966.

———. *Islam and the West: The Making of an Image.* Edinburgh: Edinburgh University Press, 1980.

De Felice, Renzo. *Jews in an Arab Land: Libya 1835–1970.* Translated by Judith Roumani. Austin: University of Texas Press, 1985.

Diop, Cheikh Anta. *Precolonial Black Africa.* Translated by Harold J. Samelson. Chicago: Lawrence Hill, 1987.

Diringer, David. *The Book Before Printing.* New York: Dover, 1982.

Dodge, Bayard. *Muslim Education in Medieval Times.* Washington, DC: The Middle East Institute, 1962.

Dozy, Reinhardt. *Spanish Islam: A History of the Moslems in Spain*. Translated by Francis Griffin Stokes. London: Chatto & Windus, 1913.

Druyan, Nitza. *Not on a Magic Carpet: Yemenite Immigrants in the Land of Israel 1887–1914*. Jerusalem: Ben Zvi Institute, 1982. [Hebrew]

Du Ry, Carl J. *The Art of Islam*. New York: Abrams, 1970.

Dwyer, Kevin. *Arab Voices: The Human Rights Debate in the Middle East*. Berkeley: University of California Press, 1991.

Dzait, Hišam. *Evropi i Islam*. Sarajevo, 1985. [Serbo-Coatian]

Elazar, Daniel J. "Sephardim and Ashkenazim: The Classic and Romantic Traditions in Jewish Civilization." *Judaism* 33, no. 2 (1984): 146–59.

Elmaleh, Abraham. *Forerunners to Zion*. Jerusalem: Rubin Mass, 1970. [Hebrew]

El Sadaawi, Nawal. *The Hidden Face of Eve*. Boston: Beacon, 1980.

Epstein, Isidore. *The Responsa of Rabbi Solomon Ben Adreth of Barcelona (1235–1310) as a Source of the History of Spain/The Responsa of Rabbi Simon b. Zemah Duran as a Source of the History of the Jews in North Africa*. New York: KTAV, 1968.

Eskandarany, Y.D. "Egyptian Jewry, Why It Declined." *Khamsin* 5 (1978): 27–34.

Fathy, Hassan. *Natural Energy and Vernacular Architecture*. Edited by Walter Shearer and Abd-el-rahman Ahmed Sultan. Chicago: University of Chicago Press, 1986.

Faur, José. "Introducing the Materials of Sephardic Culture to Contemporary Jewish Studies." *American Jewish Historical Quarterly* 63, no. 4 (1974): 340–49.

Fernea, Elizabeth Warnock. *Guests of the Sheikh*. Garden City: Anchor Doubleday, 1969.

———. *A Street in Marrakech*. Garden City: Anchor Doubleday, 1975.

Fernea, Elizabeth Warnock, ed. *Women and Family in the Middle East: New Voices of Change*. Austin: University of Texas Press, 1985.

Fischel, Walter J. *Jews in the Economic and Political Life of Medieval Islam.* New York: KTAV, 1969.

Fisk, Robert. *Pity the Nation: The Abduction of Lebanon.* New York: Simon and Schuster, 1990.

Flapan, Simha. *The Birth of Israel: Myths and Realities.* New York: Pantheon, 1987.

Franco, Moise. *Essai sur l'histoire des Israélites de l'Empire Ottoman: Depuis les origines jusqu'à nos jours.* Paris: A. Durlacher, 1897.

Friedenwald, Henry. *The Jews and Medicine: Essays and Texts.* 3 vols. New York: KTAV, 1967.

Gabbai, Mordekhai. *Whom Does the Israeli Establishment Serve?* Kfar Kadima, 1984. [Hebrew]

Galante, Abraham. *Esther Kiera.* Constantinople: Société anonyme de papeterie et d'imprimerie, 1926.

———. *Turcs et Juifs.* Istanbul: Etablissements Haim, Rozio & Co., 1932.

Geertz, Clifford. *Islam Observed.* Chicago: University of Chicago Press, 1971.

Gendzier, Irene. *The Practical Ideas of Yaqub Sanu.* Cambridge: Harvard University Press, 1966.

Gibran, Jean, and Kahlil Gibran. *Kahlil Gibran: His Life and World.* New York: Interlink, 1991.

Giladi, G.N. *Discord in Zion: Conflict Between Ashkenazi and Sephardi Jews in Israel.* London: Scorpion Publishing, 1990.

Gilman, Sander. *Jewish Self-Hatred: Anti-Semitism and the Hidden Language of the Jews.* Baltimore: Johns Hopkins University Press, 1986.

———. *The Jew's Body.* New York: Routledge, 1991.

Gilsenan, Michael. *Recognizing Islam.* New York: Pantheon, 1982.

———. *Imagined Cities of the East.* Oxford: Clarendon, 1986.

Goitein, S.D. *Jews and Arabs: Their Contacts Through the Ages.* New York: Schocken, 1955.

———. *Studies in Islamic History and Institutions.* Leiden: Brill, 1966.

———. *A Mediterranean Society*. 4 vols. Berkeley: University of California Press, 1967–1983.
Goldman, Israel M. *The Life and Times of Rabbi David Ibn Zimra*. New York: KTAV, 1970.
Goldziher, Ignaz. *Muslim Studies*. Translated by C.R. Barber and S.M. Stern. 2 vols. London, 1967–1971.
———. *Introduction to Islamic Theology and Law*. Translated by Andras and Ruth Hamori. Princeton: Princeton University Press, 1981.
Grabar, Oleg. *The Formation of Islamic Art*. New Haven: Yale University Press, 1973.
Hadawi, Sami. *Palestinian Rights and Losses in 1948*. London: Al Saqi, 1987.
Halevi, Ilan. *A History of the Jews*. Translated by A.M. Berrett. London: Zed Books, 1987.
Hamdani, Abbas. "Columbus and the Discovery of Jerusalem." *Journal of the American Oriental Society* 99, no. 1 (1979): 39–48.
———. "Ottoman Response to the Discovery of America and the New Route to India." *Journal of the American Oriental Society* 101, no. 3 (1981): 323–30.
Hassoun, Jacques, ed. *Juifs du Nil*. Paris: Sycamore, 1981.
———, ed. *Juifs d'Égypte: Images et textes*. Paris: Éditions de Scribe, 1984.
———. *Histoire des Juifs du Nil*. Paris: Minerve, 1990.
Hassoun, Jacques, Mireille Nathan-Murat, and Annie Radzynski. *Non-lieu de la mémoire, la cassure d'Auschwitz*. Paris: Éditions Bibliophane, 1990.
Hayes, J.R. *The Genius of Arab Civilization: Sources of Renaissance*. Cambridge: MIT Press, 1983.
Henry, Sondra, and Emily Taitz, eds. *Written Out of History: Our Jewish Foremothers*. Fresh Meadows: Biblio, 1983.
Hirschberg, H.Z. *The History of the Jews in North Africa*. Jerusalem: Mosad Bialik, 1965. [Hebrew]
Hitti, Phillip K. *History of the Arabs*. New York: St. Martin's, 1970.

———. *Capital Cities of Arab Islam.* Minneapolis: University of Minnesota Press, 1973.

Hodgson, Marshall G.S. *The Venture of Islam.* 3 vols. Chicago: University of Chicago Press, 1974.

Horne, Alistair. *A Savage War of Peace: Algeria 1954–1962.* Harmondsworth: Penguin, 1977.

Hourani, Albert H. *Minorities in the Arab World.* London: Oxford University Press, 1947.

———. *Arabic Thought in the Liberal Age: 1789–1939.* Oxford: Clarendon, 1962.

Hourani, George. *Arab Seafaring in the Indian Ocean in Ancient and Early Medieval Times.* Princeton: Princeton University Press, 1951.

Husik, Isaac. *A History of Medieval Jewish Philosophy.* New York: Atheneum, 1976.

Ibish, Yusuf, ed. *The Islamic City.* New York: Unesco, 1976.

Issawi, Charles. *The Fertile Crescent 1800–1914: A Documentary Economic History.* New York: Oxford University Press, 1988.

Issawi, Charles, ed. *The Economic History of the Middle East, 1800–1914: A Book of Readings.* Chicago: University of Chicago Press, 1966.

Jiryis, Sabri. *The Arabs in Israel.* Translated by Inea Bushnaq. New York: Monthly Review, 1976.

Kamen, Henry. *The Spanish Inquisition.* New York: Meridian, 1965.

Katznelson, Kalman. *The Ashkenazi Revolution.* Tel Aviv, Anakh: 1964. [Hebrew]

———. *The Ashkenazi Reckoning.* Tel Aviv: Anakh, 1989. [Hebrew]

Keddie, Nikki R., ed. *Scholars, Saints and Sufis: Muslim Religious Institutions in the Middle East Since 1500.* Berkeley: University of California Press, 1972.

Kedourie, Elie. *The Chatham House Version and Other Middle Eastern Studies.* Hanover: University Press of New England, 1984.

Kenny, Michael, and David I. Kertzer, eds. *Urban Life in Mediterranean Europe: Anthropological Perspectives.* Urbana-Champaign: University of Illinois Press, 1983.

Kerek, Ruth. *Neighborhoods in Jerusalem.* Jerusalem: Ben Zvi Institute, 1981. [Hebrew]

Keyder, Çaglar. *State and Class in Turkey.* New York: Verso, 1989.

Khalidi, Walid. *From Haven to Conquest.* Beirut: Institute for Palestine Studies, 1971.

———. *Before Their Diaspora.* Washington, DC: Institute for Palestine Studies, 1974.

———. *Palestine and the Arab–Israeli Conflict.* Beirut: Institute for Palestine Studies, 1974.

———. *All That Remains.* Washington, DC: Institute for Palestine Studies, 1992.

Khalil, Samir al-. *Republic of Fear.* New York: Pantheon, 1990.

———. *The Monument.* Berkeley: University of California Press, 1991.

Khoury, Phillip S. *Syria and the French Mandate: The Politics of Arab Nationalism, 1920–1945.* Princeton: Princeton University Press, 1987.

Kishtainy, Khalid. *Arab Political Humour.* London: Quartet: 1985.

Kroyanker, David. *Jerusalem Architecture: Periods and Styles.* Jerusalem: Domino, 1983.

Laloun, Jean, and Jean-Luc Allouche, eds. *Les Juifs d'Algérie: Images et textes.* Paris: Éditions du Scribe, 1987.

Lapidus, Ira. *Muslim Cities in the Later Middle Ages.* Cambridge: Harvard University Press, 1967.

Lapidus, Ira, ed. *Middle Eastern Cities: A Symposium on Ancient, Islamic, and Contemporary Middle Eastern Urbanism.* Berkeley: University of California Press, 1969.

Laroui, Abdullah. *The Crisis of the Arab Intellectuals.* Translated by Diarmid Cammell. Berkeley: University of California Press, 1976.

———. *The History of the Maghrib: An Interpretive Essay.* Translated by Ralph Manheim. Princeton: Princeton University Press, 1977.

Laskier, Michael M. *The Alliance Israelite Universelle and the Jewish Communites of Morocco: 1862–1962.* Albany: State University of New York Press, 1983.

———. "Albert Antebi — On His Activity in Eretz Yisrael, 1897–1914." *Pe'amim* 21 (1984): 50–82. [Hebrew]

Leon, Abraham. *The Jewish Question: A Marxist Interpretation.* Translated by D. Ferguson. New York: Pathfinder, 1970.

Levy, Reuben. *The Social Structure of Islam.* Cambridge: Cambridge University Press, 1957.

Lewis, Bernard. *The Jews of Islam.* Princeton: Princeton University Press, 1984.

Lewis, Bernard, ed. *The World of Islam.* London: Thames and Hudson, 1976.

Lewis, Bernard, and Benjamin Braude, eds. *Christians and Jews in the Ottoman Empire.* 2 vols. New York: Holmes and Meier, 1982.

Liberman, Saul. *Hellenism in Jewish Palestine.* New York: Jewish Theological Seminary, 1962.

Lustick, Ian. *Arabs in the Jewish State: Israel's Control of a National Minority.* Austin: University of Texas Press, 1980.

Maalouf, Amin. *The Crusades Through Arab Eyes.* Translated by John Rothschild. London: Al Saqi, 1984.

Mahdi, Muhsin. *Ibn Khaldun's Philosophy of History.* Chicago: University of Chicago Press, 1964.

Malek, Anwar Abdel. *La pensée politique arabe contemporaine.* Paris: Éditions de Seuil, 1970.

Mann, Jacob. *The Jews in Egypt and Palestine Under the Fatimid Caliphs.* 2 vols. Oxford: Oxford University Press, 1920–1922.

Margoliuth, David S. *Relations Between Arabs and Israelites.* London: Oxford University Press, 1924.

Mayer, L.A. *Islamic Architects and Their Works.* Geneva: Kundig, 1956.

———. *L'art juif en terre de l'Islam.* Geneva: Kundig, 1959.

Menahem, Nahum. *Discrimination and Ethnic Tension in Israel.* Tel Aviv, 1983. [Hebrew]

———. *Israël: Tensions et Discriminations Communautaires.* Translated by Michele Bitton. Paris: Éditions l'Harmattan, 1986.

Mernissi, Fatima. *Beyond the Veil.* London: Al Saqi, 1984.

Meyer, Eugene A. *Arabic Thought and the Western World.* New York: Ungar, 1964.

Miller, Ylana M. *Government and Society in Rural Palestine, 1920–1948.* Austin: University of Texas Press, 1985.

Mitchell, Timothy. *Colonising Egypt.* Berkeley: University of California Press, 1991.

Mizrahi, Maurice. *L'Egypte et ses juifs: Les temps révolu (XIXe et XXe siecles).* Lausanne, 1977.

Molho, Michael. *Usos y costumbres de los sefardies de Salonika.* Madrid: Instituto Arias Montano, 1950.

Morris, Benny. *The Birth of the Palestinian Refugee Problem, 1947–49.* Cambridge: Cambridge University Press, 1988.

Munk, Solomon. *Mélanges de philosophique juive et arabe.* Paris: J. Gamber, 1859.

Nehama, Joseph. *Histoire des Israelites de Salonique.* 5 vols. Salonika, 1954.

Neuhaus, David. *Politics and Islam in Israel 1948–1987.* M.A. Thesis, Hebrew University, 1987. [Hebrew]

Orfalea, Gregory. *Before the Flames: A Quest for the History of Arab-Americans.* Austin: University of Texas Press, 1988.

Peretz, Don. *Israel and the Palestine Arabs.* Washington, DC: The Middle East Institute, 1958.

Peretz, Nisan. *Focus East.* New York and Jerusalem: Abrams and Domino, 1988.

Persistiany, J.G. *Honour and Shame: The Values of Mediterranean Society.* London: Weidenfeld and Nicolson, 1966.

Persistiany, J.G., ed. *Mediterranean Family Structures.* Cambridge: Cambridge University Press, 1976.

Peters, F.E. *Allah's Commonweath: A History of Islam in the Near East/600–1100 A.D.* New York: Simon and Schuster, 1973.

Petuchowski, Jacob T. *The Theology of Haham David Nieto.* New York: KTAV, 1970.

Pomeroy, Sarah B. *Goddesses, Whores, Wives, and Slaves: Women in Classical Antiquity.* New York: Schocken, 1975.

Popper, William. *The Censorship of Hebrew Books.* New York: KTAV, 1969.

Rashdall, Hastings. *The Universities of Europe in the Middle Ages.* 2 vols. Oxford: Oxford University Press, 1895.

Raymond, André. *The Great Arab Cities in the 16th–18th Centuries.* New York: New York University Press, 1984.

Rejwan, Nissim. "Israel's Communal Controversy: An Oriental Appraisal." *Midstream* 10, no. 2 (1964): 14–26.

———. "The Two Israels: A Study in Europocentrism." *Judaism* 16, no. 1 (1967): 97–108.

———. "Israel's Ethnopolitical Cleavage." *Midstream* (June/July 1983).

———. *The Jews of Iraq.* London: Weidenfeld and Nicolson, 1985.

Rivlin, H.A.B., and Katherine Helmer, eds. *The Changing Middle East City.* Binghampton: Center for Social Analysis, 1980.

Rodinson, Maxime. *Islam et capitalisme.* Paris: Editions de Seuil, 1966.

———. *Israel and the Arabs.* Translated by Michael Perl. Harmondsworth: Penguin, 1980.

———. *La fascination de l'Islam.* Paris: Maspero, 1982.

———. *Cult, Ghetto, and State.* Translated by Jon Rotschild. London: Al Saqi, 1983.

Roditi, Edouard. *Magellan of the Pacific.* New York: McGraw Hill, 1973.

Rosanes, Salomon A. *Histoire des Israelites de Turquie et de l'Orient.* 6 vols. Tel Aviv, Sofia, and Jerusalem: Imprimérie "Amichpat," 1930–1945.

Rosenthal, Franz. *The Classical Heritage in Islam.* Translated by Emile and Jenny Marmorstein. Los Angeles: Near Eastern Center, UCLA, 1975.

Roth, Cecil. *A History of the Marranos*. Philadelphia: The Jewish Publication Society of America, 1932.

———. *A History of the Jews in Italy*. Philadelphia: The Jewish Publication Society of America, 1946.

———. *The House of Nasi: The Duke of Naxos*. Philadelphia: The Jewish Publication Society, 1948.

Rothschild, Jon, ed. *Forbidden Agendas: Intolerance and Defiance in the Middle East*. London: Al Saqi, 1984.

Said, Edward. *Orientalism*. New York: Vintage, 1979.

———. *The Question of Palestine*. New York: Times Books, 1979.

———. *Covering Islam: How the Media and Experts Determine How We See the Rest of the World*. New York: Routledge, 1980.

———. *After the Last Sky: Palestinian Lives*. With photographs by Jean Mohr. New York: Pantheon, 1986.

Saqqaf, Abdulazziz Y., ed. *The Middle East City: Ancient Traditions Confront a Modern World*. New York: Paragon House, 1987.

Scholem, Gershom. *Major Trends in Jewish Mysticism*. New York: Schocken, 1961.

———. *On the Kabbalah and Its Symbolism*. New York: Schocken, 1969.

———. *Kabbalah*. New York: New American Library, 1978.

———. *From Berlin to Jerusalem*. New York: Schocken, 1980.

Schonfeld, Rabbi Moshe. *Genocide in the Holy Land*. Brooklyn: Bnei Yeshivos, 1980.

Segev, Tom. *1949: The First Israelis*. New York: The Free Press, 1986.

———. *The Seventh Million: The Israelis and the Holocaust*. Jerusalem: Keter-Domino, 1991.

Sephiha, Haïm Vidal. *L'agonie des judéo-espagnols*. Paris: Editions Entente, 1977.

Shafir, Gershon. *Land, Labor, and the Origins of the Israeli-Palestinian Conflict, 1882–1914*. Cambridge: Cambridge University Press, 1989.

Shama, Abraham, and Mark Iris. *Immigration without Integration: Third World Jews in Israel.* Cambridge: Schenkman, 1977.

Shamir, Shimon, ed. *The Jews of Egypt: A Mediterranean Society in Modern Times.* Boulder: Westview Press, 1987.

Shehadeh, Raja. *Occupier's Law: Israel and the West Bank.* Washington, DC: Institute for Palestine Studies, 1985.

Shiblak, Abbas. *The Lure of Zion: The Case of the Iraqi Jews.* London: Al Saqi, 1986.

Shohat, Ella. "Sephardim in Israel: Zionism from the Standpoint of its Jewish Victims." *Social Text* 19/20 (Fall 1988): 1–36. DOI: 10.2307/466176.

———. *Israeli Cinema: East/West and the Politics of Representation.* Austin: University of Texas Press, 1989.

Sivan, Emmanuel. "Edward Said and His Arab Reviewers." *The Jerusalem Quarterly* 35 (1985): 11–23.

Slouschz, Nahum. *Travels in North Africa.* Philadelphia: The Jewish Publication Society, 1927.

———. *My Travels in Libya.* 2 vols. Tel Aviv: Va'ad haYovel, 1938–1943.

Smith, Margaret. *Rabi'a the Mystic and Her Fellow Saints.* Amsterdam: Philo, 1974.

Smooha, Sammy. *Israel: Pluralism and Conflict.* Berkeley: University of California Press, 1978.

Stillman, Norman A. *The Jews of Arab Lands: A History and Source Book.* Philadelphia: The Jewish Publication Society of America, 1979.

———. *The Jews of Arab Lands in Modern Times.* Philadelphia: The Jewish Publication Society of America, 1991.

Swirski, Shlomo. *Not Underprivileged But Made to Fail.* Haifa: Mifras, 1980. [Hebrew]

———. *Campus, Society, and State.* Jerusalem: Mifras, 1982. [Hebrew]

———. *Israel: The Oriental Majority.* Translated by Barbara Swirsky. London: Zed Books, 1989.

———. *Education in Israel: Schooling for Inequality.* Tel Aviv: Breirot, 1990. [Hebrew]

Szarmach, Paul E. *Aspects of Jewish Culture in the Middle Ages.* Albany: The State University of New York Press, 1979.

Tillion, Germaine. *The Republic of Cousins: Women's Oppression in Mediterranean Society.* Translated by Quintin Hoare. London: Al Saqi, 1983.

Toledano, Jacob. *Western Light: The History of Israel in Morocco.* Jerusalem: A.M. Lunts, 1911. [Hebrew]

Trigano, Shmuel. *La nouvelle question juive.* Paris: Gallimard, 1979.

———. *La demeure oubliée.* Paris: Lieu Commun, 1984.

Tucker, Judith. *Women in Nineteenth-Century Egypt.* Cambridge: Cambridge University Press, 1985.

Udovitch, Abraham L., and Lucette Valensi. *The Last Arab Jews: The Communities of Jerba, Tunisia.* New York: Harwood Academic Publishers, 1984.

Vajda, Georges. *Introduction a la pensée juive de Moyen Age.* Paris: J. Vrin, 1947.

Van Sertima, Ivan, ed. *Golden Age of the Moor.* New Brunswick: Transaction Publishers, 1992.

Ventoura, Moise. *La philosophie de Saadia Gaon.* Paris: Vrin, 1934.

———. *Soupirs et espoirs: Echos de la guerre 1939–1945.* Paris: Librairie Durlacher, 1948.

Watt, W.M., and P. Cachia. *A History of Islamic Spain.* New York, 1967.

Werblowsky, R.J. Zwi. *Joseph Karo: Lawyer and Mystic.* Philadelphia: The Jewish Publication Society of America, 1980.

Wolfe, Eric R. *Europe and the People without History.* Berkeley: University of California Press, 1982.

Wolfson, Harry A. *Repercussions of the Kalam in Jewish Philosophy.* Cambridge: Harvard University Press, 1979.

Wolfson, Marion. *Prophets in Babylon: Jews in the Arab World.* London: Faber and Faber, 1980.

Yerushalmi, Yosef H. *From Spanish Court to Italian Ghetto: Isaac Cardoso.* Seattle: University of Washington Press, 1982.

———. *Zakhor: Jewish History and Jewish Memory.* Seattle: University of Washington Press, 1982.

Zafrani, Haim. *Études et recherches sur la vie intellectuelle juive au Maroc de la fin du 15ᵉ siècle au début du 20ᵉ siècle*. Paris: Geuthner, 1972.

Zimmels, Hirsh K. *Ashkenazim and Sephardim: Their Relations, Differences, and Problems as Reflected in Rabbinical Responsa*. London: Oxford University Press, 1958.

Zureik, Elia. *The Palestinians in Israel: A Study in Internal Colonialism*. London: Routledge and Kegan Paul, 1979.

VI. Theoretical and Critical Sources

Adorno, Theodor. *Minima Moralia*. Translated by E.F.N. Jephcott. London: Verso, 1974.

Anderson, Benedict. *Imagined Communities: Reflections on the Origin and Spread of Nationalism*. London: Verso, 1983.

Antin, David. *Talking at the Boundaries*. New York: New Directions, 1976.

———. *Tuning*. New York: New Directions, 1984.

Anzaldúa, Gloria, ed. *Making Face, Making Soul/Haciendo Caras: Creative and Critical Perspectives by Women of Color*. San Francisco: Aunt Lute Foundation Books, 1990.

Arato, Andrew Z., and Eike Gebhardt. *The Essential Frankfurt School Reader*. New York: Urizen, 1978.

Baker, Houston A. Jr. *Blues, Ideology and Afro-American Literature*. Chicago: University of Chicago Press, 1984.

Bakhtin, Mikhail. *Rabelais and His World*. Translated by Helene Iswolsky. Cambridge: MIT Press, 1971.

Baldwin, James. *The Price of the Ticket: Collected Nonfiction, 1948–1985*. New York: St. Martin's, 1985.

Baraka, Amiri. *The LeRoi Jones/Amiri Baraka Reader*. Edited by William J. Harris. New York: Thunder's Mouth, 1991.

Baudrillard, Jean. *The Mirror of Production*. Translated by Mark Poster. St Louis: Telos, 1975.

———. *For a Critique of the Political Economy of the Sign*. Translated by Charles Levin. St Louis: Telos, 1981.

———. *Simulations*. Translated by Paul Foss, Paul Patton, and Philip Beitchman. New York: Semiotext(e), 1983.

Benjamin, Walter. *Illuminations: Essays and Reflections.* Edited by Hannah Arendt and translated by Harry Zohn. New York: Schocken, 1969.

———. *Reflections: Essays, Aphorisms, Autobiographical Writings.* Edited by Peter Demetz and translated by Edmund Jephcott. New York: Harcourt, Brace and Jovanovich, 1978.

———. *Charles Baudelaire: A Lyric Poet in the Era of High Capitalism.* Translated by Harry Zohn. London: Verso, 1985.

Benstock, Shari. *Women of the Left Bank: Paris, 1900–1940.* London: Virago, 1986.

Benveniste, Émile. *Problèmes de linguistique générale.* Paris: Gallimard, 1966.

———. *Le vocabulaire des Institutions indo-européennes.* 2 vols. Paris: Éditions de Minuit, 1969.

Bernstein, Charles, ed. *The Politics of Poetic Form: Poetry and Public Policy.* New York: Roof Books, 1990.

Bernstein, Charles, and Bruce Andrews, eds. *The L-A-N-G-U-A-G-E Book.* Carbondale: Southern Illinois University Press, 1984.

Blanchot, Maurice. "On Jabès." *Montemora* 6 (1979): 72–81.

———. *The Gaze of Orpheus.* Translated by Lydia Davis. Barrytown: Station Hill, 1981.

———. *The Writing of the Disaster.* Translated by Ann Smock. Lincoln: University of Nebraska Press, 1986.

Borges, Jorge Luis. *Labyrinths: Selected Stories and Other Writings.* Translated by Donald Yates, James Irby et al. New York: New Directions, 1964.

———. *Nuevos ensayos dantescos.* Buenos Aires: Espasa Calpe, 1982.

Cage, John. *Silence: Lectures and Writings.* Middletown: Wesleyan University Press, 1973.

Chomsky, Noam. *The Chomsky Reader.* Edited by James Peck. New York: Pantheon, 1987.

Chomsky, Noam, and Edward S. Herman. *Manufacturing Consent: The Political Economy of the Mass Media.* New York: Pantheon, 1988.

Contini, Gianfranco. *Varianti e altra linguistica*. Turin: Einaudi, 1970.

Derrida, Jacques. *Glas*. Paris: Editions Galilée, 1974.

———. *Of Grammatology*. Translated by Gayatri Chakravorty Spivak. Baltimore: Johns Hopkins University Press, 1976.

———. *Writing and Difference*. Translated by Allan Bass. Chicago: University of Chicago Press, 1978.

Dorfman, Ariel, and Armond Mattelart. *How to Read Donald Duck*. Translated by David Kunzle. New York: International General, 1984.

Dworkin, Andrea. *Intercourse*. London: Arrow, 1987.

Enloe, Cynthia. *Bananas, Beaches, and Bases: Making Feminist Sense of International Politics*. Berkeley: University of California Press, 1990.

Eno, Brian, and Russel Mills. *More Blank Than Frank*. London: Faber and Faber, 1986.

Fanon, Franz. *Black Skin, White Masks*. Translated by Charles Lam Markmann. New York: Grove Press, 1967.

———. *The Wretched of the Earth*. Translated by Charles Lam Markmann. New York: Grove, 1968.

Fischer, Michael M.J., and Mehdi Abedi. *Debating Muslims: Cultural Dialogues in Postmodernity and Tradition*. Madison: University of Wisconsin Press, 1990.

Fletcher, Angus. *Allegory: Theory of a Symbolic Mode*. Ithaca: Cornell University Press, 1982.

Foster, Hal, ed. *The Anti-Aesthetic: Essays on Post-Modern Culture*. Port Townsend: Bay, 1983.

Freud, Sigmund. *Moses and Monotheism*. Translated by K. Jones. New York: Vintage, 1955.

———. *On Creativity and the Unconscious*. Translated under the supervision of Joan Riviere. New York: Harper and Row, 1958.

Geertz, Clifford. *The Interpretation of Cultures*. New York: Basic Books, 1973.

hooks, bell. *Yearning: Race, Gender, and Cultural Politics*. Boston: South End, 1990.

Jacobs, Jane. *The Death and Life of Great American Cities*. New York: Random House, 1961.

Jones, LeRoi. *Blues People*. New York: William Morrow, 1963.

———. *Home: Social Essays*. New York: William Morrow, 1966.

Kelly, Joan. *Women, History, and Theory*. Chicago: University of Chicago Press, 1984.

Kubler, George. *The Shape of Time*. New Haven: Yale University Press, 1962.

Lévinas, Emmanuel. *Quatre lectures talmudiques*. Paris: Editions de Minuit, 1966.

Lukács, Georg. *The Theory of the Novel*. Translated by Ann Bostock. London, 1971.

Mackey, Nathaniel. "Sound and Sentiment, Sound and Symbol." *Callaloo* 30 (Winter 1987): 29–54.

Mandelstam, Osip. *The Complete Critical Prose and Letters*. Edited by Jane Gary Harris and Constance Link. Ann Arbor: Ardis, 1979.

Mariani, Philomena, ed. *Critical Fictions: The Politics of Imaginative Writing*. Seattle: Bay, 1991.

Meddeb, Abdelwahab. "Lieux/Dits." *Les Temps Modernes* 375 (October 1977): 21–45.

Memmi, Albert. *The Colonizer and the Colonized*. Translated by Howard Greenfeld. New York: Orion, 1968.

Metcalf, Paul. *Genoa*. Penland: The Jargon Society, 1965.

Minh-ha, Trinh T. *Woman, Native, Other*. Bloomington: Indiana University Press, 1989.

———. *When the Moon Waxes Red*. New York: Routledge, 1991.

Olson, Charles. *Human Universe and Other Essays*. Edited by Donald Allen. New York: Grove, 1967.

———. *The Special View of History*. Edited by Ann Charters. Berkeley: Oyez, 1970.

Olson, Tillie. *Silences*. New York: Delacorte, 1979.

Palmer, Michael. *Code of Signals: Recent Writings in Poetics*. Berkeley: North Atlantic, 1983.

Perloff, Marjorie. *The Poetics of Indeterminacy: Rimbaud to Cage.* Evanston: Northwestern University Press, 1984.

Reed, Ishmael. *Writin' Is Fightin'.* New York: Atheneum, 1990.

Reinhardt, Ad. *Art as Art: Selected Writings.* Edited by Barbara Rose. New York: Viking, 1975.

Scarry, Elaine. *The Body in Pain: The Making and Unmaking of the World.* New York: Oxford University Press, 1985.

Scully, James. *Line Break: Poetry as Social Practice.* Seattle: Bay, 1988.

Showalter, Elaine D., ed. *The New Femininst Criticism: Essays on Women, Literature, and Theory.* New York: Pantheon, 1985.

Stillman, Ron. *The New Sentence.* New York: Roof Books, 1987.

Simmel, Georg. *On Individuality and Social Forms.* Edited by Donald N. Levine. Chicago: University of Chicago Press, 1971.

Simonson, Rick, and Scott Walker, eds. *Multi-Cultural Literacy: Opening the American Mind.* St. Paul: Greywolf, 1988.

Smith, Barbara. *Home Girls: A Black Feminist Anthology.* New York: Kitchen Table, 1983.

Solomon, Maynard, ed. *Marxism and Art: Essays Classic and Contemporary.* New York: Vintage, 1974.

Thompson, Robert Farris. *Flash of the Spirit: African and Afro-American Art and Philosophy.* New York: Vintage, 1984.

Walker, Alice. *In Search of Our Mother's Gardens.* New York: Harcourt, Brace, and Jovanovich, 1983.

Wallace, Michele. *Invisibility Blues: From Pop to Theory.* New York: Verso, 1990.

Wallis, Brian, ed. *If You Lived Here: The City in Art, Theory, and Social Activism — A Project by Martha Rosler.* Seattle: Bay, 1991.

Walton, Ortiz M. *Music: Black, White, and Blue.* New York: Morrow Quill, 1972.

Whorf, Benajmin Lee. *Language, Thought, and Reality.* Cambridge: MIT Press, 1956.

VII. Journals, Periodicals, and Additional Reference Works

Journals and Periodicals

'Afiqim [Hebrew]
BeMa'arakha [Hebrew]
Encyclopedia of Islam
Encyclopedia Judaica
Hebrew Union College Annual
'Iton Aher [Hebrew]
The Jewish Encyclopedia
Jewish Quarterly Review
Journal of Arabic Literature
Journal of Modern Hebrew Literature in Translation
Journal of Palestine Studies
Khamsin
Levant: cahiers de l'espace mediterranéen
Mediterraneans
MERIP *Reports*
Pe'amim [Hebrew]
Prooftexts
Revue des Études Juives
Shevet ve'Am [Hebrew]
Les Temps Modernes
The Universal Jewish Encyclopedia

Additional Reference Works

Betsalel, Itshak. *The Writings of Sephardi and Oriental Jewish Authors in Languages Other Than Hebrew: A Bibliographical Survey of Belles Lettres in the Twentieth Century.* Tel Aviv: Tel Aviv University and the Center for the Integration of the Oriental Jewish Heritage, 1982.

Cohen, Hayyim J., and Zvi Yehuda. *Asian and African Jews in the Middle East, 1860–1971/Annotated Bibliography.* Jerusalem: Ben Zvi Institute, 1976.

De Rossi, Giovanni Bernardo. *Dizionario Storico degli Autori Ebrei e delle Loro Opere.* 2 vols. Parma, 1802.

Kayserling, Meyer. *Biblioteca Española-Portuguesa-Judaica.* Edited by Yosef H. Yerushalmi. New York: KTAV, 1971.

Moreh, Shmuel. *Arabic Works by Jewish Writers: 1863–1973.* Jerusalem: Ben Zvi, 1973.

www.ingramcontent.com/pod-product-compliance
Lightning Source LLC
Chambersburg PA
CBHW051132160426
43195CB00014B/2445